PRAISE FOR

THE RECURRENCE EFFECT

"If you value curiosity and candor, this book delivers. Perry Maughmer gives you a simple, honest rhythm for returning to what matters most and becoming someone you trust. Perry Maughmer invites you to stop performing, get honest, and come back to yourself. The Recurrence Effect helps you recognize where you have drifted and choose who you want to become."

—RYAN HAWK,
bestselling author & host of *The Learning Leader Show*

"*The Recurrence Effect* is built atop a powerful insight: Drift—not failure—is the true enemy of a meaningful life. Maughmer shows how to overcome that drift not through contemplation, but through action."

—DANIEL H. PINK,
#1 New York Times bestselling author of *The Power Of Regret* and *Drive*

"Practical and honest, *The Recurrence Effect: A Rhythm for Returning to What Matters Most* asks the kinds of self-reflective questions that wake us up to how we're showing up—and whether our focus is aligned with what truly matters. Perry invites us to live with awareness and purpose that deepens our capacity to serve others."

—SAM REESE,
CEO, Vistage Worldwide

"*The Recurrence Effect: A Rhythm for Returning to What Matters* doesn't hand you answers, it hands you the mirror. In these pages, Perry Maughmer confronts the "drift," reclaiming your agency, helping you walk through the fire that forges the evolving you. It is not a roadmap however; it is a reckoning, an invitation to intentionally design the life you want and deserve. If you're looking for self-help, this isn't that either. This work is a guide to self-authorship for anyone brave enough to trade performance for presence, and drifting for deliberate becoming. Powerful, piercing, and refreshingly honest, Maughmer shows you how to stop performing the life others expect and start creating the one you were made for. Most books promise transformation, this one demands it. Prepare to confront the truth and burn what no longer belongs, to rise into the life you've been avoiding but longing for. Thanks to Perry, I now understand that real change doesn't wait for clarity, it meets you in motion."

—**MARK PANCIERA,**
CEO Emeritus, Partner at The Pacific Institute High-Performance Mindset Expert TEDx/YPO Speaker

"*The Recurrence Effect* isn't a book you finish—it's a book you return to. Perry Maughmer offers a rare blend of courage, compassion, and clarity, inviting us to stop performing our lives and start inhabiting them. This is not self-help. It's self-honesty—and it's exactly what our restless world needs. This is a mirror, not a map—and it may be the most honest book you read this year."

—**GREG CLEARY,**
Founder Pinnacle Business Guides, Author of *Peak Performance*

"Read this if you truly care about how you are moving through the world—as a person, as a leader, as someone committed to evolving. Perry has a rare ability to see what most of us miss, especially the truths just outside where we think we're supposed to focus. From the moment I met him, I was struck by his clarity—not loud or performative, but steady and precise. This book doesn't cheerlead. It witnesses. 'Here's the thing: You don't need cheerleaders. You need witnesses—people who will not allow you to lie to yourself in front of them.' This whole book is that, if you let it be. My copy is full of highlights because Perry says things just differently enough to create those audible ah moments—the kind that subtly but meaningfully shifts how you see yourself and the world. Do not read this if you prefer the comfort of the status quo. Read it if you're ready to reassess, readjust, and stop drifting."

— HILARY BLAIR,
keynote speaker (CSP), champion of human connection, and the CEO of ARTiculate: Real&Clear

THE RECURRENCE EFFECT

A RHYTHM FOR RETURNING TO WHAT MATTERS MOST

PERRY MAUGHMER

Story **BUILDERS** PRESS

The Recurrence Effect: A Rhythm for Returning to What Matters Most
Copyright © 2026 Perry Maughmer

No part of this book may be reproduced or transmitted in any form or by any means, electronic or mechanical, including photocopying and recording, or by any information storage or retrieval system, except as may be expressly permitted by the Copyright Act of 1976 or in writing from the publisher. Requests for permission should be addressed to storybuilderspress@gmail.com.

Published by StoryBuilders Press
Paperback: 979-8-89833-046-0
Hardcover: 979-8-89833-047-7
eBook: 979-8-89833-048-4

FOR LISA, MY WIFE AND FIRST WITNESS

You lived with the rough drafts of this long before any of it made its way to paper. You held the fragments, the false starts, the doubts, and the wandering. And still, you reminded me—gently, relentlessly—that the only work worth doing is the work we return to. Again and again.

FOR ZANE, ZACH, AND GRACE

The ones who walked beside me while I tried to build the bridge beneath my own feet. You are the quiet reason behind every sentence. Your love keeps me honest. Your presence keeps me grounded. Your belief keeps me returning.

FOR MY PARENTS, DEANE AND KAYE

You gave me a beginning shaped not by words but by example: work done without applause, humility worn without performance, and the steady truth that character is built in the unseen hours. You taught me that the world doesn't owe us ease—only the chance to show who we are. Thank you for giving me a foundation strong enough to stand on, push against, and grow beyond.

FOR MY SISTER, LISA

You shaped the way I see the world—the good, the hard, the beautiful, the honest. Your life revealed a truth I have spent decades trying to articulate: we don't choose our path, but we do choose how we walk it. And sometimes courage is nothing more than being seen and continuing anyway.

TABLE OF CONTENTS

Prelude: This Book Is a Mirror, Not a Map 1

PART I: EXPLORE 13
Chapter 1: The Drift You Didn't Notice 15
Chapter 2: The Stories That Were Never Yours 35
Chapter 3: This Moment Will Not Come Again 49

PART II: EXPERIMENT 63
Chapter 4: You Can't Think Your Way into a New Self 65
Chapter 5: The Biology of Becoming 87
Chapter 6: The Collapse of the Mask 101

PART III: EVALUATE 121
Chapter 7: Reflection Is Where Meaning Begins 123
Chapter 8: No One Grows in Straight Lines 141
Chapter 9: Alignment Is a Daily Act of Courage 155

PART IV: EDIT 179
Chapter 10: Your Identity Isn't a Fact; It's a Draft 181
Chapter 11: The Pain of Precision 201
Chapter 12: Become Someone Worth Returning To 223

Afterword: Longing, Discovery, and Reckoning 239
Epilogue: The End of the Beginning 247
Endnotes 250

PRELUDE

THIS BOOK IS A MIRROR, NOT A MAP

The mass of men lead lives of quiet desperation.
HENRY DAVID THOREAU

What would it take for you to be happy—to feel like you've finally made it?

Go ahead and think about that for a moment. Maybe it's a promotion at work, starting your own business, or hitting that seven-figure mark.

It could be personal achievements—weight loss, graduation, or running a marathon. Or it could be relationship goals.

I'll let you in on a little secret: Whatever outcome you're dreaming of or striving to achieve, it will never be enough.

THE RECURRENCE EFFECT

If all your dreams came true overnight, you might feel happy and fulfilled for a day or two. But those feelings wouldn't last. Before long, you'd be back wondering what it would take to reach the finish line.

But there is no finish line. It's a mirage. And deep down inside, we know it.

Yes, we love goals and outcomes. We nearly worship achievement and chase clarity like it's some kind of prize. But we will never arrive and reach fulfillment because there is no arrival.

In fact, the belief that achievements are the source of happiness and satisfaction is a cognitive bias called *the arrival fallacy*. It is just one of more than 180 cognitive biases that affect the way we process information, perceive the world around us, and make decisions.[1]

Author and teacher Tal Ben-Shahar describes the arrival fallacy as expecting lasting fulfillment from achieving our goals. But as we all know, the satisfaction we experience from achievement is fleeting. That is because our brains adjust quickly and our exciting new reality becomes our boring new status quo. And so we start chasing the next achievement that promises to fulfill us but won't.[2]

The good news is that there's a way to get off of this dopamine-chasing hamster wheel. And it starts with realizing that happiness, fulfillment, and satisfaction are not end goals. They aren't the pot of gold at the end of the rainbow.

Instead, they are found in the work we do, in our experiences, and in who we become through them. As Ralph Waldo Emerson wrote, "Life is a journey, not a destination." In life, there is only our effort and how it shapes us.

And it's the process, not the outcome, that actually edifies us.

THIS BOOK IS A MIRROR, NOT A MAP

WHAT THIS BOOK ISN'T

Let me say this clearly right up front. This is not a leadership book.

It's not about becoming a better manager. It's not about climbing a corporate ladder or building influence or owning a room.

This is a book about how you live, how you move through the world, how you show up when it counts, and how you act when no one's watching. And if that resonates even just a little bit, then this is for you. Really, it's for all of us.

Before we go any further, let me say the following. I don't have this all figured out. This isn't my memoir from the mountaintop. I didn't write this because I've mastered everything. I'm not an expert. I'm a witness, and I'm in this with you.

But here's my warning: If you're looking for a system or a tidy little model to help you get better, this isn't it. This isn't a set of hacks. It's not about self-improvement.

This book isn't here to help you look better. You're not going to get motivation porn. You're not going to get self-help jargon. And you're definitely not going to get any shortcuts to being a better leader, gaining confidence, or getting a promotion. You're not going to get any of those because that's not what you or I or anyone else needs.

You don't need to follow someone else's path for validation. You don't need to *look* better; you need to *live* better—not in someone else's eyes or by their rules but by your own, because this is *your* life, not somebody else's. The path you're on is yours and yours alone, and no one else can walk it. And no one can tell you *how* to walk it.

This is your journey, your odyssey. It will use something I call Explore, Experiment, Evaluate, and Edit (4E). It isn't a process. It's a rhythm, a lived cadence of exploration, experimentation, evaluation, and editing. That's how we evolve. That's how we wake up. We explore what we believe, we experiment with how we show up, and we evaluate what our actions reveal. And then—the part most of us miss—we *edit*. We cut what no longer serves. We refine what aligns. We rewrite the next draft of who we are. That isn't something we do once or for a season. It's the rhythm we return to again and again for as long as we're alive.

I wrote this book because this is how I live every day. It's actually an exploration of what goes on inside my head.

It's a field report from the middle of the nasty mess because I needed to make sense of what it means to live and lead in a way that's honest, and I couldn't do it alone.

This book is that sense-making out loud. So when I say this is for all of us, I mean it.

Throughout the book, I will encourage you to sit with what you're uncovering about yourself and who you're becoming. Those reflections are not meant for seeking clarity, finding answers, or aligning yourself with someone else's path. They are about how you show up for yourself and how you interact with the world around you.

This practice of reflection comes from a philosophy called *existential phenomenology*. For the purposes of this book, you don't need to know a lot about existential phenomenology, but there are a few things it would be helpful for you to understand.

Phenomenology focuses on exploring and investigating events (phenomena) through as unbiased a lens as possible, free of preconceptions and external interpretations.[3] One branch of this philosophy, existential phenomenology, seeks to understand experiences by analyzing the experience itself.[4]

That's what I am inviting you to do as you reflect.

THIS BOOK IS A MIRROR, NOT A MAP

Before that, I want you to start with your own body and what's going on inside of you. That is called interoception—your ability to sense your own internal state. It is not just awareness or presence but a deep literacy, a fundamental knowledge of your being. If you can't feel what's happening inside of you, you can't trust yourself. And if you can't trust yourself, why should anyone else?

We don't lead from theory. We lead from embodiment. Although our society tries to separate our head or our minds from the rest of our bodies, it's impossible because physiologically it's all connected. You are a whole person—mind and body. And you have to be that whole person in order to evolve.

So here's a prompt for embodiment. Close your eyes and think about the following questions:

- Where is the tension in your body right now?
- What's underneath that sensation?

Don't try to fix it. Don't judge it. Just notice it.

That's the beginning of the process. Take stock of yourself before moving further.

WHAT THIS BOOK IS

Now that we've covered what this book is not and what you won't get from it, here's what you will get. You'll get provocation. You'll get really raw questions, and you'll get a process that prompts you to keep calling out your own nonsense because that's the first step to evolving—becoming aware of it.

But I want to be clear. This isn't about adding items to your to-do list.

THE RECURRENCE EFFECT

It is literally a reckoning, not with your role or with your job. It's a reckoning with the version of yourself you've learned to perform and whether that version serves who you are becoming. The process won't be easy, but it will be real, and it will be honest.

How comfortable are you with honesty? We're often very good at telling the truth to other people, but we're not always very good at telling the truth to ourselves. Honesty is the only place evolution can actually begin.

We have to be willing to take an unfiltered, honest look at ourselves—to ask how we're truly showing up for ourselves and which version of us we're offering to the world in every part of our lives.

I get that you may not want to accept what you discover about yourself because sometimes the truth is heavy. I get it. Again, this isn't going to be easy, but it will be honest. And what's real and honest is what will endure.

The process of honest Exploration, Experimentation, Evaluation, and Editing will look different for each of us. We're each on our own path, our own odyssey. Just like Ulysses was on his odyssey, not anybody else's, we can't follow somebody else's path as if it were our own.

There are millions of self-help books on the shelves that promise success if we follow steps one, two, and three or do seven things before 5:00 a.m. or whatever was on that author's path to fulfillment. And that's the key, by the way—*their path*. No doubt what they did worked for them, and that's awesome. But that's their journey, not yours or mine. The real work can't be outsourced. Each of us has to face our own. That's where the hard part begins.

Each of us has to do the work of forging our own path. There's no way around it. There's no hack. There's no shortcut because no one else's path is made for you. Philosopher Friedrich Nietzsche

THIS BOOK IS A MIRROR, NOT A MAP

pushes the weight of responsibility even further, writing, "No one can build you the bridge on which you, and only you, must cross the river of life. . . . There is one path in the world that none can walk but you. Where does it lead? Don't ask, walk!"[5]

It would be like trying on someone else's custom-made clothing and expecting it to fit you equally well. The clothing would likely be functional. You could probably wear it, but it would never feel right. Those clothes would never fit you and your life because they were made for someone else. You just have to find your own fit.

Again, this process isn't about a new checklist to follow or about learning how to do things my way. This isn't about adding stuff in; it's about peeling something back. You don't need to become someone new. You need to remember who you were before you began performing for others. Hopefully, this book will help you remember.

As you begin to rediscover who you are and how you want to move in this world, don't forget that your self is the very core of the work. Your career or whatever you do for a living is secondary.

The process has to impact everything you do, everything you are. That's the only way you can expect a different result.

Now, take a moment and pause. Ask yourself where you are in the process right now in the rhythm of Exploring, Experimenting, Evaluating, and Editing

- What am I Exploring with curiosity and not control?
- What am I trying not to win but to see?
- What did my last success or failure reveal about who I'm becoming?
- What do I need to put down in order to make room for something more meaningful?

HOW TO READ THIS BOOK

This process, like life, is not a solo journey. We can't do this on our own.

This isn't just about personal growth; it's about shared impact because you can't and you don't evolve in isolation. You need people.

You need people to hold you accountable. You need people to challenge your story. You need people to reflect to you who you said you wanted to be. And when I say reflect, they're holding up that mirror to you and reminding you what you said you wanted.

Here's the thing: You don't need cheerleaders. You need witnesses—people who will not allow you to lie to yourself in front of them.

We seek out cheerleaders because it makes us feel good, but that's not what we need. We need open, honest, caring witnesses—people who are willing to tell us the truth. Have you ever actually said the words *please tell me the truth* and then acted in a way that aligned with that request? If you're not hearing the truth, it's often because of the way you react to the truth. Do you truly want to hear it?

Throughout this book, I'll offer you four mirrors to show you where you are. I call them mirrors because they're not for validation; they're for truth.

Mirrors, in all their glory, don't lie to you. They don't offer an opinion. They simply reflect what the light reveals if you're willing to look. Here are the three mirrors I'll offer you.

- *The Judgment Curiosity Spectrum:* Shows where are you defending old, false stories about yourself and where you are open to seeing what's real

THIS BOOK IS A MIRROR, NOT A MAP

- *The Gratitude Challenge Grid:* Reflects what's anchoring you, what matters, and what's pressing you to grow

- *The Learning-Knowing Mirror:* Reveals where you're gathering information to feel certain versus engaging experience to create understanding

- *The Edit Filters Matrix:* Clarifies what to keep, what to cut, and what's worth returning to so your choices align with who you're becoming

This process is not about balance; it's about becoming. And the mirrors are merely reflections during the process. They are simply for a status check so you can orient yourself and determine where you want to go from here. Orientation is part of the process, and it's central for us.

To orient yourself, you need two pieces of information: where you are right now and where you are headed. These will point you in the direction you need to go. Remember that we are focused on our direction and our journey, not our destination. That's really important.

So let's pause for another reflection. Allow yourself to sit with any tension you may be feeling as you consider where you are and where you want to be.

- What am I bringing to this work? Am I willing to be seen here, or am I still pretending?

- What parts of me am I scared to let surface?

- Who will be impacted when I stop performing?

THE RECURRENCE EFFECT

REDEFINING LEADERSHIP

As we pursue this rhythm of Explore, Experiment, Evaluate, and Edit, let me give you an example of what I mean by reckoning. We've been told that leadership is something you earn, that it's a role, a position, or a title. But here's the shift I want to suggest. Leadership is not who you are. Leading is something you do, and I'll tell you how I define it.

Leading is making the world a better place for those you care deeply about. That's it.

It's not to create followers. It's not for applause. It's not for more money. It's not for a better position. It's not to prove something.

We lead because we care. We can recommit to it. If leading is just a label, it becomes almost like armor that keeps the truth out.

But since leading is an activity and not a title, we can get better at it. We can reflect. We can recalibrate. This book is not about *becoming* a leader. It's about practicing the act of leading deliberately, courageously, and repeatedly.

Leading is an action—a verb, never a noun.

Going back to the definition of leadership, we're creating a better world for those we care deeply about. Whoever is on that list for you, I want you to look at those people and the impact you have on them.

Here's our next reflection. Pause and consider.

- Who am I becoming when I think about leading? Do I see it as a role or a responsibility?
- Where have I been performing leadership instead of practicing presence?
- Who are the people I care deeply about, and how am I showing up for them?

THIS BOOK IS A MIRROR, NOT A MAP

NEXT STEPS: MOVING FORWARD

If you're still with me, then maybe you're ready. That doesn't mean you're ready like "prepared and have everything together." That's not what I'm talking about. I'm asking you if you are willing to shed all the performing and pretending. Are you ready to feel your way forward? Are you ready to tell the truth?

Henry David Thoreau wrote that he went to the woods because he wanted "to live deliberately, to front only the essential facts of life, and see if I could not learn what it had to teach, and not, when I came to die, discover that I had not lived." Instead of living a life of quiet desperation, he "wanted to live deep and suck out all the marrow of life."

That's what I'm inviting you to do.

I want to reinforce that I am not outside of this process. I'm in this every day. I have been actively focused on employing this rhythm for the last five years. That has been central to my life, and I have barely scratched the surface of what's possible.

I'm excited and energized by that because I talk about the Relentless Few. As the saying goes, "All can, most won't, few do." The tagline for the Relentless Few is this: "We're done when we're dead."

Isn't that empowering, exciting, and energizing? We have the rest of our lives to Explore, Experiment, Evaluate, and Edit. And it is a blessing to be able to do that because we have the opportunity to continually evolve.

So please forget the checklist.

Forget the titles.

Forget the myth that anyone else has your answer for you.

No one is coming to save you. And that is awesome news because *you never needed it*. You are the answer, and you always have been.

Now let's begin.

PART I
EXPLORE
(WITH CURIOSITY)

CHAPTER 1

THE DRIFT YOU DIDN'T NOTICE

The greatest hazard of all, losing one's self, can occur very quietly in the world, as if it were nothing at all.

SØREN KIERKEGAARD

Ask yourself this: Where am I really going, and when did I stop deciding for myself?

Drift is dangerous, and it can be very subtle. Imagine you're on a hike through the woods or sailing on the ocean. You set out on your journey with a purpose and a direction in mind because without those, there is a good chance you'll end up lost or in trouble. Even when you're prepared, there's still a risk of getting off course if you're not paying attention.

THE RECURRENCE EFFECT

Every journey has its own inherent pitfalls. When you're hiking, you may think you're safe because you're following a well-maintained trail. But if you haven't stopped to consider if the path actually leads where you want to go, you may find yourself miles down the trail, going in the wrong direction.

Sailing is a different kind of journey. There aren't always clearly marked paths to follow, and the danger is in outside forces—storms, winds, currents—that push you off course. If you don't regularly check where you're headed, you may discover that your trajectory has shifted away from what you intended.

That is what we refer to as drift. It might be almost imperceptible at first, but each small deviation pushes you farther and farther from where you want to be and where you want to go.

In this chapter, I'll open the door for a kind of reckoning in your life. Again, I'm not offering a road map but instead a rupture or a pattern interruption. The drift you didn't notice isn't just a chapter title. It's a callout because most of us didn't consciously choose the version of ourselves we're currently living.

All too often, we've arrived where we are right now through accumulation or momentum, through roles and actions we said yes to without considering or remembering why. That is drift.

Drift is what happens when we outsource our becoming. It's a slow, quiet surrender of our agency. It's not a choice, not really; it's the absence of one. But it's not laziness, and it's not weakness. It's the default. Drift is expected and normal. Without a clear answer to "What do I want most?" we become adrift because we're unmoored. When we don't have a port to sail to, any wind blowing in any direction is favorable.

It's the result of never stopping to ask, "Who am I becoming?"

The brutal truth that accompanies this is that if we don't consciously choose the path we want to be on, drift chooses it for us. Recognizing the drift in our lives isn't really about changing anything. It's about seeing—really seeing—and seeing is the most dangerous act of all because once you see, you can't unsee.

Once you've chosen to look at where you are and where you're headed, you will see where drift has taken you, what paths you've inherited, and what version of yourself you're showing to the world. Then you can ask if those things serve you, if they serve something beyond yourself, and if they serve those you care deeply about.

That's the first step toward self-transcendence.

EXISTENTIAL SELF-TRANSCENDENCE

You may be familiar with the concept of self-transcendence in the context of Maslow's hierarchy of needs. Just briefly, Abraham Maslow's initial hierarchy outlined five levels of human needs that are necessary for development, growth, and well-being. They include physiological needs (food, water, shelter, and rest), safety needs (security and stability), love and belonging needs (relationships, affection, and connection), esteem needs (self-respect and recognition from others), and self-actualization needs (personal growth and realizing your full potential).

In a later version, Maslow added self-transcendence at the top of the hierarchy. In Maslow's model, self-transcendence sits above self-actualization as the highest human need. It's not about fulfilling our own potential for ourselves. Instead, it is focused on serving something bigger than ourselves. It's a purpose or a cause such as the future or the people we care deeply about.[6]

That type of self-transcendence is motivational. It pulls us through hardship because the goal is not personal comfort but impact. It's relational. It's not just about becoming *you* but about becoming *for* others.

It's purpose-driven. You're not climbing a mountain to plant your own flag but to help others climb and plant theirs.

Maslow saw self-transcendence as the only sustainable course of motivation for continued growth because once you've self-actualized, there's a risk of stagnation and self-centeredness. For ongoing flourishing, you have to move past yourself, your needs, and your goals. That is what I mean when I say things like "What I want most is not for *myself* but for *others*." We evolve because we owe it to others, not just ourselves.

There is a second type of self-transcendence I'll talk about in this book. It's self-transcendence according to existential phenomenology, the experience of going beyond. Here the term is less about a goal and more about a felt experience that moves beyond the immediate confines of the self.

That kind of self-transcendence includes a type of flow experience, like the moment we're so absorbed in creating that we forget ourselves. It's the moment we break a long-held personal pattern and experience spaciousness. It's the visceral call to respond that we feel when we witness suffering. It's when we stop performing and just sit with someone else in truth.

Self-transcendence like this is not structured, goal-oriented, or moralized. It's about experiencing the self as more than a fixed identity. It's fluid; it's relational; it's becoming. It's part of stepping out of the default you've inherited or built out of survival and stepping into the possibility of becoming.

When I talk about self-transcendence, I don't just mean serving others. I mean evolving in a way that makes service possible. Maslow gives us the target to go beyond ourselves in the name of others, but the real, messy work happens moment by moment. It's when you notice the drift, resist comfort, and return to what you believe matters most.

THE DRIFT YOU DIDN'T NOTICE

Maslow's model tells us why we must transcend the self to serve. Existential self-transcendence unfolds in lived experience and the struggle to return again and again to what matters most.

The work you must do is grappling with inherited scripts, facing drift, reckoning with what you want most, and moving from self-actualization to self-transcendence. That's the interior path to becoming someone capable of making a difference beyond yourself. This isn't about being selfless. It's about becoming *more* than the self you've been so you can give something real to those you care about.

The first step toward existential self-transcendence is trading the things that soothe us, that allow us to drift, for what matters most to us. We have to identify our drift and move away from what I call emotional novocaine, making life comfortable at the expense of our growth and evolution.

The rhythm of Explore, Experiment, Evaluate, and Edit begins not with motion but with orientation. To orient yourself successfully, you need two points: where you are and where you want to go. Your direction should be determined by what matters most to you. That is where you want to go. To get there, you have to be completely honest with yourself about where you are.

That's typically where individuals and even organizations fall short. We may be clear on where we want to go, and we'll sit around and talk about what we want most, but then we're not honest and open with ourselves about where we're starting from. We like to imagine that we're farther along than we are or that we haven't already drifted off course.

So we have this gap between where we are and where we want to believe we are. Then we create a plan, and of course, the plan doesn't work because we haven't oriented ourselves to the correct starting point.

THE RECURRENCE EFFECT

NAMING THE DRIFT

As you orient yourself, and if you're honest about where you are and where you want to go, you will begin to see how drift is affecting you. Drift is how most of us end up where we are.

Remember, drift is what happens when we outsource our becoming. It's not laziness. It's not weakness. It's the cost of never asking this question: "Who am I becoming?"

By default, drift is the slow accumulation of choices from obligation, not alignment. It's the momentum of other people's expectations dressed up as our own ambition. It feels familiar. So we confuse it with what we really want to do and be, and we drift farther out of alignment with ourselves.

Nature abhors a vacuum, so if we don't clearly decide what we want most, others—our family, society, and friends—will decide for us. Again, I'm not saying that following others' decisions is necessarily bad. It's just that allowing others to decide what matters most to us keeps us from making our own choices.

Drift is insidious because we don't notice it at first. It's not an abrupt turn. It's not a 180-degree or even a 90-degree shift. It's like the tiniest shift in our trajectory when we don't realize we're drifting away from who we are and where we want to go until we get to the point that we don't recognize ourselves anymore. At some point, we wake up and discover we're monumentally off course.

Drift isn't failure; it's unconscious conformity to someone else's expectations. German philosopher Martin Heidegger said, "Everyone is the other, and no one is himself."[7] And that's what's so dangerous about drift. Slowly, almost imperceptibly, we lose ourselves and become who others want us to be.

But the moment we notice, the moment we become aware, the moment we wake up, we create the possibility to go beyond

THE DRIFT YOU DIDN'T NOTICE

it. That possibility is the first flicker of existential self-transcendence. Identifying and naming the drift only happens if we pause long enough to ask, "Am I chasing what I want *most* or just what I want *now*?"

To withstand the distraction, the urgency, and the fear that is pushed upon us—the drift—we have to know deeply and fundamentally what we really want most.

THE JUDGMENT CURIOSITY SPECTRUM

In this part of the book, we will be focusing on the first "E" of the Explore, Experiment, Evaluate, and Edit rhythm. Part of becoming aware of drift in your life is seeing what is real—who you really are, where you want to go, what you really want most—and recognizing the old, false stories about yourself that no longer serve you.

The mirror I want to offer you as you begin the process of Exploration is the Judgment to Curiosity Spectrum.

JUDGMENT					CURIOSITY
CONDEMNATION	CRITIQUE	SKEPTICISM	ACCEPTANCE	INQUIRY	WONDER
Extreme Judgment	Evaluative Judgment	Cautious Inquiry	Acknowledging Difference	Active Exploration	Open Curiosity

A fluid continuum, not a moral ladder.

The Judgment to Curiosity Spectrum reflects fluid and ongoing movement among mindsets rather than a linear progression from "bad" to "good." The goal is not to reside permanently at one end or the other but to develop awareness of where we are at any given moment and understand how to move consciously along the continuum as needed.

THE RECURRENCE EFFECT

Our position on this continuum not only shapes our internal experience but also significantly impacts those around us. Being mindful of how our mindset affects others can deepen our connections and foster a more intentional presence.

Beginning on the Judgment end of the spectrum, we have Condemnation, an extreme form of judgment. Condemnation is a rigid and absolute stance where differing perspectives are seen as inherently wrong or misguided. There's no space for Exploration or understanding, which leads to quick dismissal or outright rejection. This stage often arises from a need for certainty and control.

Condemnation often has a negative impact on others. It creates defensiveness and withdrawal since people feel judged or belittled. It shuts down open dialogue, leaving others feeling unheard and undervalued. It also damages trust since others sense a lack of empathy and openness.

Here is one question to ask yourself to determine if you are positioned in Condemnation right now: "When was the last time I truly listened to someone I disagreed with?" If you find yourself feeling dismissive of others or pushing for certainty, pause and ask yourself, "What might this reaction be communicating to those around me?"

And take the time to sit with the answers.

Next on the Judgment to Curiosity Spectrum is Critique, or evaluative judgment. In this position, the focus is on identifying flaws or inconsistencies, often in a way that feels rational or analytical. While there's more engagement here than Condemnation, the primary intent is still to find reasons to discredit rather than understand.

Like Condemnation, Critique tends to negatively impact those around us. It makes people feel scrutinized rather than understood, which leads to guardedness. It erodes psychological safety as people may fear critique rather than feeling valued. And it reduces collaboration since others may hold back ideas to avoid judgment.

The question to reflect on is this: "Am I more focused on finding flaws than on exploring new ideas?" Before critiquing, consider how your feedback might influence the other person's willingness to share in the future.

As we move away from Judgment toward Curiosity, the third position is Skepticism, or cautious inquiry. Skepticism is a transitional stage marked by a willingness to question your own assumptions while still feeling somewhat guarded. There's a cautious openness to new ideas, but it often feels tentative or hesitant.

Skepticism's impact on others is somewhat mixed. It signals that you are open to dialogue, but you may still come across as hesitant to fully engage. On the one hand, it encourages some exploration, but on the other hand, people may sense a lack of full commitment to understanding. Skepticism may create a space for conversation, but it may not feel entirely safe or supportive.

If you find yourself in skepticism, ask yourself, "Am I open to the possibility that I might not have the whole picture?" That question will help you move toward greater curiosity and away from judgment. When you acknowledge aloud that you feel unsure or conflicted, it can humanize your stance and invite others to share openly.

Fourth on the Judgment to Curiosity Spectrum is Acceptance, or acknowledging difference. Acceptance means recognizing that multiple perspectives can coexist without feeling threatened. It's not about agreement but about holding space for differing viewpoints without rushing to resolve or judge them.

Acceptance tends to have a positive impact on those around us. It builds trust since others feel their viewpoints are respected. It also creates a foundation for more authentic dialogue since people sense that they won't be dismissed, and it encourages a culture of inclusivity where differences are seen as valuable.

The question to reflect on here is this: "Can I acknowledge the validity of a perspective different from my own without feeling threatened?" To build acceptance, practice verbalizing how you will accept differing views without necessarily agreeing. You could try saying, "I see how you might see it that way, even if my experience is different."

Moving closer to the Curiosity end of the spectrum, the next position is Inquiry, or active exploration. Inquiry involves actively seeking to understand different perspectives with genuine curiosity. It's characterized by asking thoughtful questions and being open to having your own beliefs challenged.

Inquiry inspires openness and reciprocal curiosity since people feel invited to share more deeply. It builds psychological safety since others feel valued and respected. It also encourages collaboration since people sense a shared commitment to learning.

Here is a reflective question for Inquiry: "What can I learn from this perspective, even if it challenges my own?" From a position of Inquiry, you can begin conversations with a question that shows genuine interest in the other person's viewpoint, such as, "Can you share more about how you came to that conclusion?"

The final position on the Judgment to Curiosity Spectrum is Wonder, or full curiosity. Wonder reflects a state of openness and fascination that embraces ambiguity and the complexity of human experience. There's no rush to label, categorize, or resolve, but rather a willingness to dwell in Exploration.

Wonder has an overall positive impact on others. It fosters a deep sense of belonging since people feel genuinely seen and valued. It cultivates a culture of innovation since ideas flow without fear of judgment. Wonder also inspires vulnerability since others feel safe to share their authentic selves.

As you reflect on Wonder, ask yourself, "What if I allowed this new idea to challenge my current beliefs?" When you are feeling curious, express it openly: "I hadn't thought of it that way before; tell me more about your perspective."

REFLECTION PAUSE

Before continuing to the next section, I encourage you to pause and consider the following thoughts. Be sure to take some time to sit with your answers to the questions. Feel the tension between who you are right now and who you want to become.

👁 AWAKEN

- Where in your life are you performing in line with choices you never actually made?
- When did you last feel truly awake in your own life, and what pulled you back into drift?

📍 REMEMBER

- You didn't consciously choose everything you're currently carrying. That doesn't mean you have to keep holding it.
- The drift isn't failure. It's forgetting, and now you're remembering.

> **← RETURN**

- What one assumption about who you are do you need to question today?
- How could you interrupt one unconscious pattern—not to fix it but to feel it?

NAVIGATING THE JUDGMENT TO CURIOSITY SPECTRUM

Movement along the Judgment to Curiosity Spectrum is natural and context-driven. Instead of striving to always be at the Curiosity end, the objective is to build awareness of where you are and recognize the impact your current mindset has on others. Embrace the fluidity of the continuum.

There are moments when Judgment may serve a purpose—safety or discernment—just as there are times when Curiosity is essential for connection and growth. Being mindful of your position on the continuum helps you make more intentional choices about how you show up for others.

This is important because Judgment interferes with the three Ls that matter in life: loving, learning, and leading. Leading is not organizational or professional. It's about creating a better world for those we care deeply about. Judgment keeps us from loving, learning, and leading. We can only do them when we're curious, because Judgment stops everything. Nothing grows out of Judgment. Where Judgment shames, Curiosity invites. Judgment is terminal, but Curiosity is transformational.

Curiosity is about more than reflection; it's the posture required for transcendence. We cannot move beyond the self while clinging to certainty. For example, Judgment would say, "Why did I waste so much time?" whereas Curiosity asks, "What led me here, and what can I learn from it?" One position shuts down growth and exploration; the other encourages them.

Before we can move from Judgment to Curiosity in our interactions with others, we have to start with understanding how we can do so for ourselves internally. If we address ourselves with curiosity and the voice in our head isn't so judgmental of ourselves, then that same curiosity and lack of judgment will flow from us toward others.

Reflect on these two options: "Why did I waste so much time?" or "What led me here, and what can I learn from it?" Think about the emotional states these internal questions create within yourself. They are very powerful things.

This is also the place to ask, "If I'm not sure what I want most, how can I know if this version of me is serving it?" And recognize that what you want most will change. It's never final; it's never static. It's always evolving.

And so we have to keep returning to the question in different phases of our lives because the answer will evolve. We have to continually reorient ourselves to fight against drift.

SLEEPWALKING TOWARD IDENTITY AND WAKING UP

When we allow external forces and other people's expectations to shape who we are and what we want, we end up sleepwalking toward our identity. It's passive and unintentional. It's outsourcing our becoming. It does not reflect what we want most, even when it looks like we're successful.

Drift often looks like success because it aligns with the arrival fallacy. Good things happen even as we drift. We get promoted.

THE RECURRENCE EFFECT

We hit our numbers. We're praised for consistency and showing up. That is the arrival fallacy in action. We want to believe that we'll finally feel fulfilled once we reach some external milestone.

But what happens when we get the title, the salary, the house, and the recognition? Our kids will go to the right school, and we'll get the country club membership—whatever the goal might be. The reality is that no matter what the achievement, we're still restless because our happiness gauge resets.

An external measure of happiness will never last, and nothing external will fill that hole inside of us, despite what our consumeristic culture says. Our culture feeds us constant messages—you deserve this treat, you deserve this car, you need this vacation and all the "good things" in life. The underlying implication is that if you get this thing or do that thing, you'll be happy.

But that's just categorically untrue. And you know that deep down.

Every time I ask people this question, I get the same response and the same head nod: "When have any of those things ever made you happy?" When you have the house, the salary, the title, the car, the deal, or whatever you want—when you have all of them and say, "I'm done now; I'm finally happy," is it ever enough?

No matter who I ask, the answer is always the same. The happiness and satisfaction never last, and nothing is ever enough.

Danish philosopher and theologian Søren Kierkegaard wrote, "The greatest hazard of all, losing one's self, can occur very quietly in the world, as if it were nothing at all."[8] When you chase what culture rewards instead of what your soul requires, the cost is your very self. Think about what Kierkegaard was saying, that losing one's self happens gradually, quietly, and imperceptibly. Drift slowly accumulates over hundreds of microdecisions. But then so does transcendence.

THE DRIFT YOU DIDN'T NOTICE

I want to encourage you to take the first micro-action toward transcendence by asking, "What am I chasing?" What's the first pattern you are going to interrupt? Are you willing to do what it takes? Do you want to be accountable and responsible? Do you want to understand the power you have to choose at every moment because the choice is always yours?

Do you want to wake up? Then it's time to act, and it begins with your body.

We don't *think* our way out of drift. We *feel* our way back to ourselves. We have to reconnect the mind with the body. We have forgotten how to understand what our body tells us. We've bought into the belief that logic and impassivity are good, and thus we cut ourselves off from feeling and emotion. We want to think our way through everything without paying attention to what the body tells us. But our bodies and minds are not enemies.

Your body and your mind are connected, both part of one organism—you. And science proves that. In our brains, areas that control movement, thinking, planning, and autonomic processes (breathing, heart rate) overlap.[9] What we think, do, and feel are interconnected.

Our bodies give us signals through our emotions and physical feelings, but we suppress and learn to ignore them because we believe that we should be unemotional, which is a whole lot of nonsense. Our emotions and feelings are very important. They shouldn't drive our behavior, but they are *indicators* to us that *something* is going on. We have to listen to our bodies' signals because our bodies carry our stories.

Have you ever been in a meeting or situation where you felt a tightness in your chest or your jaw clenching? What about periods of sleeplessness, shallow breathing, or sweating when you're facing challenges? How do you respond to those signals in your body?

THE RECURRENCE EFFECT

All those experiences are indicators that we tend to ignore or dismiss as "just stress," which is really detrimental to our overall well-being. As French philosopher Maurice Merleau-Ponty explained, "The world is not what I think, but what I live through."[10] Our experiences matter. What we feel matters. Therefore we cannot and we must not arbitrarily separate our minds and our bodies.

We have to get back into our bodies. We have to develop our skills of interoception, our perception of what is happening in our bodies.[11] We have to be able to understand what our bodies are telling us. Interoception reconnects us to our present reality, and that is a gateway to transcend the unconscious patterns we've embodied.

As we improve our interoception, we have to ask questions like these:

- Where in my body am I still holding someone else's expectations?
- What sensations have I learned to ignore?
- Where have I tuned out from listening to my body's signals?

When we tune out our bodies, we lose our instincts and the indicators that dramatically impact us and help us understand ourselves in the context of our current moment. Ask yourself, "What might my body say about what I want most if I gave it room to speak?"

We know that when we experience feelings and emotions, even when we ask questions or make statements, our brains don't feel anything. It's our bodies that feel. When we feel something that aligns with who we are, we feel our soul exhale, and we feel connection. That's our bodies doing that, not our brains. And we must reconnect the two.

THE DRIFT YOU DIDN'T NOTICE

REBELLION AND THE PRACTICE OF RETURN

Seeing clearly and asking these questions of yourself is subversive. It's the refusal to drift silently. French philosopher Albert Camus is credited with saying, "The only way to deal with an unfree world is to become so absolutely free that your very existence is an act of rebellion." And the world does not want you to rebel.

It wants participation. It wants consumption. It wants all the things. It does not want you thinking and feeling freely. It does not want you asking those questions of yourself and then making decisions that align with the answers.

Rebellion isn't easy, but it's necessary for transcendence.

Transcendence begins when we stop playing the parts we didn't audition for, the parts that do not serve who we are and what we want most. We start by taking a break and truly answering the questions.

Rainer Maria Rilke summarized what I mean when he wrote, "Be patient toward all that is unsolved in your heart and try to love the questions themselves . . . [L]ive everything. Live the questions now. Perhaps you will then gradually, without noticing it, live along some distant day into the answer."[12] Exploration is done through lived experiences. We can't just think about these questions. We have to *live* them.

- What roles have you been playing on autopilot?
- Who benefits from your silence, your numbness, and your drift?
- Who or what is currently defining what you want most?
- Are you defining it, or is someone else?

These questions and this book are meant to challenge you, not condemn you. I invite you to this Exploration from a position of curiosity, not judgment. I want this process to open you up to possibility.

I'm not telling you who you should be. I'm showing you how you got here and how you can return to who *you* are and whatever *you* decide is most important to you. That is where self-transcendence begins, not in a perfect plan but in a pause, in a choice to see. That choice is always guided by deeper knowing—knowing what you want most.

Just as the tendency to drift is constant, so must our return be—and not just once. We must return again and again. This is the rhythm of recurrence. The difference is that where drift is unconscious survival, return is conscious reorientation, and recurrence is deliberate devotion to returning over time.

Drift is passive and linear. Return is interruptive and reflective. Intentional recurrence is rhythmic, selected, and chosen. It does not just happen.

	TRIGGER	NARRATIVE	ENERGY SOURCE
Drift	Avoidance	"This is just how things are."	Inertia
Return	Discomfort	"Something isn't right."	Awareness
Recurrence	Practice	"This matters, and I'm willing to return again."	Commitment

Here's how to recognize and name drift. Drift is triggered by avoidance, over-identification, and autopilot. It's the story we tell ourselves that "this is just the way life is." And it's driven by inertia, doing nothing and making no conscious changes.

THE DRIFT YOU DIDN'T NOTICE

In contrast, the trigger for return is discomfort and disillusionment. It's that moment of clarity when we recognize that something isn't right. That awareness is what motivates us to stop drifting and return to what we want most.

Each time we return, we move toward recurrence, which begins with practice, pattern, and promise. We remind ourselves what matters to us and what we're willing to return to again and again. Our commitment to what matters most drives us to stop drifting and continue returning.

That is the rhythm of drift, return, and recurrence, which leads to transcendence. The answer to the question "What do I most want?" is the baseline that keeps us from drifting and getting lost in the noise around us. We have to establish that baseline so we can return to it, which brings us back to ourselves. That's what a base line does in music. It keeps the rhythm.

Author Anaïs Nin wrote, "What we call our destiny is truly our character, and that character can be altered."[13] What she meant is that there's no permanence to our personality. Who we are, our character, and our destiny are not hardwired, but they need to reflect what we want most over the course of our lives.

Drift is what happens when we forget who we are and what we want most—when we avoid and when we hide. Return is what happens when we remember. And recurrence is the rhythm of returning again and again, which reveals what we want most because we *are* what we return *to*.

RETURN FROM THE DRIFT

Remember that becoming is never a done deal. It's never static. It's never final. And it's not meant to be. You aren't stuck. You don't need to be fixed. We are beginning our Exploration with curiosity, not judgment. So be gentle with yourself as you sit with these questions and the tension inside you.

👁 AWAKEN

- Who benefits from your staying asleep to your own becoming?
- What part of you has been waiting for permission to make a different choice?

📍 REMEMBER

- Drift thrives in the absence of attention. But awareness is always available.
- This isn't about fixing your life; it's about reentering it with your eyes open.

↩ RETURN

- What part of your rhythm no longer fits the person you're becoming?
- How will you create one moment tomorrow that feels like a return, not a reaction?

Now that you're aware, now that you're awake, you're ready to move on to the next chapter where we will learn to ask if the stories we believe about ourselves are really our own.

CHAPTER 2

THE STORIES THAT WERE NEVER YOURS

We are unknown to ourselves.

FRIEDRICH NIETZSCHE

When you look in a mirror, whose reflection are you really seeing?

That seems like an obvious question. Of course, you see your own reflection in the mirror. But sometimes we don't see just ourselves. Have you ever gotten a glimpse of yourself and thought, "Wow, I look like my dad"? Or maybe you've been told you have your grandfather's nose or your mom's eyes.

We inherit physical characteristics, personality traits, and health risk factors from our biological families. Even if you grew up in a family without shared DNA, you have likely acquired mannerisms, family dynamics, and belief systems from the people who raised you. That's normal. A significant part of who we are comes from our families and communities.

We are also shaped by the stories we learn from our families such as family myths, cultural scripts, and narratives that are passed down like family heirlooms we never ask for. Most of us live without ever questioning those inherited beliefs inside us. They feel natural to us, until they don't.

What are the stories in your life that were never really yours?

This is the moment I invite you to name them. I want you to step out of the default self you've inherited or built out of survival and step into the possibility of becoming.

This isn't about what to do; it's about what to unbelieve. It's identifying and letting go of the stories that no longer serve who you are and what you want most. This is a critical step toward self-transcendence.

As we talked about in the last chapter, this transcendence isn't Maslow's moving beyond ourselves in service to others. This is the self-transcendence that is not structured, goal-oriented, or moralized. It's about experiencing the self as more than a fixed identity. It's the self as fluid, relational, and becoming.

Maslow's transcendence gives us the reason. Phenomenology gives us the path and shows us *how* that transcendence actually unfolds in a lived experience. It's the struggle to return again and again to what matters most. That's what we're talking about here. We will revisit these ideas throughout the book as we return to essential concepts and fundamental questions. That's on purpose because I want to show you how the return to recurrence works.

Returning is the activity; recurrence is the rhythm. We need to keep returning to these foundational things and revisiting them, not just continuing to add and add and add. Returning is necessary because we see things differently when we return because we are not the same person we were the last time we experienced it. In this chapter, we are sitting in the tension between "what I want now" and "what I want most."

Because our beliefs were handed to us, so were our definitions of things such as success and goodness. If we never question those beliefs and definitions, we may spend our entire lives chasing what we want *now* without ever asking what we want *most*. My hope is that this chapter will help you begin to separate that signal from the noise.

STORY AS STRUCTURE AND CAGE

We are meaning-making machines. That's not my opinion, and it's not optional. It's science; it's scientific fact. Our brains make up our stories. Our brains really don't want us to think. They want us to use scripts, worldviews, and paradigms—whatever we want to call them—as lenses to see the world through and as a way to make decisions quickly about the world around us.

Your brain doesn't want you to think deeply and see anything differently. It wants to categorize things rapidly to save energy because evolutionarily, your brain wants to reduce the time spent thinking about things. That will solve problems and create stories for you more quickly than you can imagine.[14]

We have to understand that reality and start making it central to our questioning, because what your brain uses to make meaning are these things that are *inherited* more than *chosen*. They are the stories that actually give shape to who you think you are, what you believe you deserve, and what you think is possible, acceptable, or realistic.

Here's the twist. Most of these stories—these paradigms, these worldviews—were written by someone else. We got this framing from our family of origin's expectations, our religious or moral coding, our education, and our community. It's how we learn to define things such as gender roles, success metrics, and cultural default settings. All these things were provided to us.

Ask yourself these questions:

- Who taught me how to define good, success, fun, fair, or right?
- Where did I learn those ideas?
- Where did I learn what work is supposed to feel like?
- What's my earliest memory of being told who I am?

That last question is one to really sit with. Who told you who you are? How often?

We have inherited and accepted those early stories, shaping the self we learned to survive as. We don't really know who we are because as German philosopher Friedrich Nietzsche wrote, "We are unknown to ourselves."[15] We have never searched for ourselves. But our self-transcendence begins by questioning the very scaffolding or understanding of that self and by asking, "Did these stories ever serve what I wanted most or just what I needed to survive at the time?"

THE ORIGIN OF INHERITED SCRIPTS

Inheriting worldviews or belief systems is perfectly normal. Everyone has them. They are part of our development. The rhythm of exploring—evaluating and questioning who we are and what we want most—is not about right or wrong, good or bad.

Going back to our Judgment to Curiosity Spectrum, we have to ensure that we're sitting in the wonder or full-curiosity position, or at least in inquiry. We can't interrogate these stories from judgment. If we do, we'll blame others. We'll shame ourselves and shut down. We want to move away from the Judgment end of the spectrum—acceptance, skepticism, critique, condemnation—and be in the Curiosity end of that continuum because that's where we're able to consider questions.

From a position of judgment, exploring our inherited stories is going to sound something like "I should be over this by now." But if you begin from a place of curiosity, it will sound more like "Why did this story feel true for so long?" And those questions bring up very different emotional and physical responses.

The Judgment to Curiosity Spectrum is essential in this chapter because without it, you will stay armored—guarded against evolution. The rhythm—Exploration, Experimentation, Evaluation, and Editing—requires softness, a necessary condition for growth beyond what was handed to us. We have to let curiosity shape *how* we explore, not just *what* we explore.

Existential transcendence demands not just confrontation but compassion. Curiosity also invites a deeper inquiry into questions such as this: "Is this story keeping me focused on what I want now or freeing me to pursue what I want most?" When we're sitting in curiosity, our approach to exploration is softer and more compassionate.

Before continuing, reflect on where you are currently positioned on the Judgment to Curiosity Spectrum and move toward Curiosity if you're not already there.

Now that we know where our inherited stories or scripts come from, we will consider how those narratives take hold. We absorb beliefs before we develop discernment, the perception and absence of judgment we need to obtain understanding. The prefrontal cortex of our brains where all our executive decision-making takes place does not fully develop until we're in our late teens or early twenties, generally earlier for women than for men.[16]

Innovation, creativity, and discernment—all our decision-making—take place in that part of our brain. Physiologically, we are incapable of having access to all that until our brains finish developing. And so when we're younger, we absorb all those beliefs without questioning because we actually can't question them yet. We weren't designed to do that from an evolutionary standpoint.

There's absolutely nothing wrong with the fact that we inherited stories and worldviews from our families, our religious communities, our schools, and our neighborhoods. Nothing wrong happened. Nobody did anything to us they weren't supposed to do. We needed someone to provide us with an understanding of the world and ourselves because we weren't capable of doing it ourselves. We had to have sense-making mechanisms and paradigms given to us by those close to us. There was no way around it. The challenge now is this: What do we do with them?

As kids, we needed coherence, logic, and consistency more than truth. We needed something to depend on. We couldn't actually investigate or really understand truth the way we can as adults. The danger, though, is that what protects us in childhood calcifies in adulthood. If we're not careful, it solidifies, and we never stop and ask, "Do these things still serve us?"

Here's an example of an inherited story that serves us as children but can hinder us as adults: "If I'm quiet, I stay out of trouble." As we're growing up and learning, it's not a bad idea to stay out of trouble and learn to listen. However, that same story for adults can lead to beliefs like this: "If I don't speak up, I can't be wrong," and "If I succeed, I'll finally be loved."

When you ask a group of adults their opinions, ideas, or insights about something, most of them get quiet. They're looking for the "right" answer because they don't want to be "wrong." They were conditioned throughout their schooling to only speak if they knew the "right" answer. However, as we've discussed, for our exploration, there is no right or wrong answer, but that conditioning runs deep.

Jean-Paul Sartre said, "Man is nothing else but what he makes of himself."[17] Too often we make ourselves out of someone else's materials. We're not looking internally and building ourselves. We are taking what was given to us, and those are the materials we base our evolution on. We never stop to question what is truly inside of us.

The interesting thing is that these stories may never have been true, but they carry truth about us. Albert Camus is credited with saying, "Fiction is the lie through which we tell the truth." The challenge now is to discern what stories still serve the self we're willing to become. (Again, nothing wrong was done to us. There is no judgment or condemnation in asking these questions.)

What matters now is whether or not we will stop and ask ourselves what still serves us and recognize the power of discernment that we have now as adults. Are we willing to explore, experiment, evaluate, and edit what we entered adulthood with and what we're going to continue with?

No matter your age, the stories about who you are and what you want most—even the inherited ones you choose to continue with—are always fluid. Going back to self-transcendence, you always want to be actively moving beyond yourself based on what you're learning and understanding.

That's why you have to have this constant return. You have to have the rhythm of recurrence because you need to keep coming back to these questions and answers. Self-transcendence will ask, "What must I unlearn to return to what I want most?" That's the question because learning—rooted in curiosity—allows for fluid movement.

THE RECURRENCE EFFECT

Knowing—positioned in certainty—limits learning. You have to understand and accept that the more you *know*, the less you *learn*.

REFLECTION PAUSE

Before continuing to the next section, I encourage you to pause and answer the following questions. Be sure to take some time to sit with your answers. It's okay to feel unresolved tension or discomfort as you explore the stories that were never yours.

👁 AWAKEN

- What beliefs did you inherit before you even had the language to question them?
- Which parts of your identity were shaped by survival, not intention?

📍 REMEMBER

- You didn't choose the original story, but you've been the main character in it ever since.
- Safety once required performance. Growth now demands honesty.

↩ RETURN

- Where in your life are you still playing a role that no longer fits?
- What truth have you avoided because it threatens the story you've always told?

THE STORIES THAT WERE NEVER YOURS

CONFRONTING THE COST

As we explore our inherited stories, we don't just name them. We name the cost of carrying them. Some of those costs include what the stories have kept you from trying and how they have shaped your relationships and even yourself. Consider what parts of you have gone silent because they didn't "fit the narrative."

Martin Heidegger reminds us, "Every man is born as many men and dies as a single one." At birth, our possible futures seem limitless. As we age, the options narrow over time unless we actively intervene in our own evolution. Existential self-transcendence begins when we question what that narrowing has excluded.

Do not abandon your past. Instead, hold it up and ask, "Is this mine?"

If it's not, are you willing to put it down to become more than you have been?

That's all part of the rhythm of Explore, Experiment, Evaluate, and Edit. We'll talk more about each of these later, but this is evaluating and editing. When you're willing to ask, "Is this aligned with what I want most? Is it serving me and those I care deeply about?" you begin to evaluate. Remember, nothing is bad or wrong. You're not judging yourself or your answers; you're simply asking and evaluating. And then you have to be willing to edit.

You have to put down things that aren't going to serve you in order to pick up things that do. You can't just keep adding and adding and adding to your load. You have to remove the things that are keeping you from what you want most.

Here's where we should return to interoception, embodiment, and emotional resonance. What's going on in your body while you explore your inherited stories? We talked in the previous chapter about having a somatic awareness of our physical responses because our stories live in our bodies. We have to be in tune with and understand our bodies.

Maybe you feel a tightness in your jaw, your chest, your shoulders, or your neck when you're challenged. Maybe your breathing gets shallow when you start to think about speaking up in a meeting, that kind of shallow breathing we get as a little bit of anxiety starts to wash over us. Or maybe your shoulders tense up every time you say yes when you mean no.

Those are sensations and feelings we have to recognize. We don't just *think* our stories; they show up in our bodies, and we can't ignore those signals. Maurice Merleau-Ponty said, "We know not through our intellect but through our experience." Transcendence is not a thought; it's a felt shift.

You need to reconnect with the part of you that was forced to adapt to other people's expectations and beliefs. Only then can you begin to return to who you are and who you want to be. As you work on improving interoception, you can ask yourself this:

- What belief does this tension in my body reflect?
- What story is my body still rehearsing?
- Is my body living a story that contradicts what I want most?

Your body is giving you important information. You just need to be aware. You need to sit with it. You need to understand it. You need to acknowledge it, and you need to question what it's coming from. You need to recognize when you start to feel a certain way and ask, "Why do I feel this way?" Again, it's without judgment.

When you ask yourself what led you here and what made your body react, the questioning is enough to release you. You don't necessarily need an answer. You just need to accept that maybe what you're feeling in your body is caused by a story you're running that isn't serving you anymore.

TOWARD DISCERNMENT, NOT ERADICATION

Let's pause for a moment. I want to be clear. I'm not telling you to throw out everything you've ever believed or to get rid of all your inherited stories. That's not what I'm after. You're not starting over from scratch; you're building discernment.

Discernment is part of the sacred editorial aspect of transcendence. It's how we become who we are *meant* to be, not just who we were *told* to be. Those are not binary decisions or sweeping 180-degree turns. We're not just flipping a switch or changing our clothes.

That's not the kind of change we're after. Changes like that are not a sustainable approach to becoming who we are meant to be. We are evolving, and it's sacred because we have to discern what parts we're keeping and what parts we're editing. We're learning to interpret the world through who we are and who we are becoming. As Anaïs Nin said, "We don't see things as *they* are, we see them as *we* are."

Transcendence isn't the rejection of our roots. It's the refusal to remain rooted in a soil that no longer nurtures who we are becoming. And that's really important. We're not saying everything was bad. Nobody did anything wrong. Your family, teachers, coaches, and community leaders didn't do anything wrong. You didn't do anything wrong.

You're simply understanding that you would like to become a version of yourself that will serve you and create a better world for those you care about. To become who you are meant to be, you have to be willing to evolve. American psychologist Rollo May wrote, "The opposite of courage in today's society is not cowardice but conformity."[18] Courage comes from refusing to conform to stories, worldviews, paradigms, and beliefs that do not support your evolution.

Are the stories you're still living aligned with what you want *now* or what you want *most*? Again, that's a simple question, and I want you to just sit with it without judgment. These stories are not *you*. They're stories that either serve you or don't.

Stories are not hardwired. They aren't immovable or unchangeable. They are not facts. They're merely ways to understand yourself and the world around you. You hold onto them because you find them comfortable or easier than exploring and discerning. The stories do live within you, but now you get to choose what lives on. And that's really hard.

Discernment is not a one-time decision. It's not one and done. That's why we call this "the recurrence effect" because we have to keep coming back. We have to keep getting in that rhythm, returning to the things that matter, and returning to these questions. As Rainer Maria Rilke told a young poet, "Live the questions now."[19]

As you step deeper into exploration, be gentle with yourself. Pay attention to your body and what it's telling you. The questions are not to judge you or provoke you. Instead, I want to encourage you to start unhooking your inherited identity from who you are meant to be so you can create space for transcendence.

You aren't empty or starting over from nothing, but you are filled with outdated stories like a computer with old programming. Once you edit out the parts that no longer serve you, you get to write something new, something that aligns with what you want most. So write like it matters because it definitely does.

THE STORIES THAT WERE NEVER YOURS

RETURN FROM THE DRIFT

The ancient myth of the phoenix is that it burns itself up and then rises out of the ashes. Like the phoenix, the process of evolution is painful but rewarding. Use the following questions to help you identify stories that were never yours.

👁 AWAKEN

- What story is your body still rehearsing—without your consent?
- Are the beliefs you live by aligned with what you want now or what you want most?

📍 REMEMBER

- You are not broken—you are burdened by stories that were never fully yours.
- These stories were useful once, but they are not sacred.

↩ RETURN

- What inherited script are you finally ready to put down?
- What new truth do you need to speak, even if your voice shakes?

Remember, we don't experience this process in a vacuum. We never do it alone. We do it in the context of witnesses. In the next chapter, we'll explore why the present is the time for change.

CHAPTER 3

THIS MOMENT WILL NOT COME AGAIN

No man ever steps in the same river twice, for it's not the same river and he's not the same man.

HERACLITUS

How much of your life is spent thinking about and planning for the future?

When the kids go to college, we'll take that trip we've always talked about. After I finish this project at work, I'll prioritize my personal development. If I just keep my head down and do good work, the right people will notice.

THE RECURRENCE EFFECT

The problem is that all these plans rely on the "myth of later." We tend to live our lives with the deeply ingrained delusion that life begins at some point in the future after certain benchmarks are met. We've been conditioned to believe that now—the present—is just a stepping stone, that this moment is just preparation for a future moment that matters more.

But what if *this* is the moment that matters most?

Ichigo ichie, a concept that originated in the Japanese tea ceremony, literally means "one time, one meeting." The words remind us that "what we are experiencing right now will never happen again."[20] It's the same reminder of the transient nature of life that we see in the quote by Heraclitus at the beginning of this chapter. We can never step into the same river twice. We only have the present moment, and it will not come again.

We are now in the only place where change is possible—in this present moment. I don't mean that in a sentimental way. I mean it as a dare or a challenge to confront the impermanence of our world. This chapter is about presence, not in the sense of mindfulness or a productivity technique but as the foundation of truth at the beginning of self-transcendence.

You can't edit your life, rewrite your stories, or reclaim your agency if you're not fully present in your life. That's because the present is the only point of power you have. It's the only thing that truly exists and the only place you have any power to do anything. You can't change the past, and the future hasn't happened yet.

As we discussed in the first two chapters, you are sitting in the tension between what you want most and what you want now. This is the moment where those two collide. If you're not fully present, you will default to what you want now. But if you return to what you want most, you can reclaim your agency and your choice over the moment you're in right now.

THIS MOMENT WILL NOT COME AGAIN

To return, to evolve, and to achieve self-transcendence you have to stop—stop running, stop rationalizing, and stop distracting yourself long enough to see what's really here. Be present in this moment and then the next one and the next one. You have to realize that "later" is a myth.

In his book *Being and Time*, Martin Heidegger wrote about temporality, an existential concept about how the future shapes the meaning of the now. We always project ourselves into the future even when we think about being present, and we live in anticipation to the point that it's only in the face of our death that we find meaning. Our finality gives time its weight.

When we talk about presence, it's about recognizing our limited horizon and choosing to live in a way that aligns with our deepest concern. That is what Heidegger described as authentic temporality.[21] Authentic temporality is not just moving through time. It's choosing how to live within time because you know how it will end.

Going back to what you want most versus what you want now, authentic temporality is only possible if you're completely anchored in what you want most. If you're clear on that, you can make the necessary choices to live each moment, but if you aren't, you can't.

You're always able to choose who you're becoming. Every moment is a moment that you could have lived differently and that can haunt you unless you own it. When you're consciously choosing to be in the now, you can make choices without fearing regret.

Time is not a prison; it's a portal to self-transcendence. The present moment in time is the only place you have power to choose who you will become and for whom. If you understand the fluidity of yourself, of who you are, then you continually get to choose.

This moment doesn't wait, and it won't come again. That isn't a productivity tip. It's an existential fact. You don't have forever. And that's what makes this moment matter.

That means presence isn't passive. It's how you begin to live beyond yourself toward something greater than control or comfort. It only happens when you stop living for what you want now and begin orienting toward what you want most.

ATTENTION VS. THE LOOP OF DISTRACTION

What we pay attention to reveals what we actually value, not what we say we value. Where does your attention go when you're tired? What do you turn to when you're uncomfortable? What do you avoid noticing in your daily life?

French philosopher Simone Weil wrote, "Attention is the rarest and purest form of generosity."[22] I want to invite you to see attention as moral, existential, and intimate because if you're not giving attention to this moment, you're not living. You're scrolling or browsing through life.

If your attention is always captured by what soothes you right now, how can you ever build toward what matters most? Being distracted by what soothes you is like emotional anesthetic, numbing you from life's tensions and discomforts.

Being present and giving your attention to someone is an existential act and something you can't do 100 percent of the time. It would be exhausting, and I'm not advocating for that. Presence is about choice. It's about noticing and choosing when to give our attention fully.

Life is heavy. So sometimes the reason we scroll, binge, or distract ourselves is because we're avoiding the weight of what's real. I'm not saying we should carry that weight all the time, but when something heavy needs our attention, avoiding it only adds to the burden.

Presence isn't all or nothing. It's not about being fully present all the time. It's about recognizing the moments that matter and choosing to show up for them. And when we *do*, we *are*.

The digital world we live in makes being present a challenge. We have the ability to access all things all the time. We feel a need to document everything instead of experiencing it. Often we're not present in the moment because we're always recording the moment. We're taking pictures and doing things that share the moment instead of being *in* the moment. We lose the ability or the desire to know that some moments don't need to be recorded.

It reminds me of a scene from the movie *The Secret Life of Walter Mitty* with Ben Stiller. Sean Penn's character is Sean O'Connell, a wildlife photographer who's trying to get a picture of a snow leopard referred to as the "ghost cat." Stiller, as Walter Mitty, finds O'Connell sitting there with his camera, huddled down with snow all over him. When O'Connell looks through his camera, he sees it. It is right in the frame. Stiller asks why he doesn't take the picture, and O'Connell says, "Sometimes I don't. If I like a moment, for me, personally, I don't like to have the distraction of the camera. I just want to stay in it."[23] When we live in the past or in the future, we end up living with regret or future fantasies. We're not living in the present, and we're not really experiencing life. And that is a natural, predictable result of the cognitive biases we've incorporated to simplify our thinking.

Our brain is wired to keep us safe. That's the number one priority: Keep us safe so we can procreate. That's how our brains work. Our brains aren't designed for presence. They are designed for survival in an unpredictable, dangerous environment.

THE RECURRENCE EFFECT

We have a Stone Age mind in a modern skull, and that's the struggle. We're not living in that world anymore. What helped us stay alive as hunter-gatherers now keeps us stuck in the cycles of distraction because our brain is a threat-detection device.

It's all part of our evolutionary wiring. That is not a moral failure. Nobody's to blame. There is no shame in having cognitive biases. They aren't bad; we need them. They evolved to allow us to react quickly to situations. The challenge is to identify them and choose when to allow them to work and when we should not.

There are three cognitive biases we need to be aware of as we choose presence: negativity bias, present bias, and attentional bias. Negativity bias means we constantly scan for threats and assume everybody's a threat or an enemy until proven otherwise. When we look at the world, we see threats, not gifts. The present moment is rarely seen for what it offers, only what it might lack. When we create stories about our world, about the way somebody's behaving, we never default to the positive. We default to the negative.

Present bias leads us to prioritize what we believe are the costs and benefits of our choices right now. It reinforces our decisions to pursue what we want (or don't want) now instead of what we really want. This is a kind of living *for* the moment that is not the same as living *in* the moment. Presence is not about instant gratification but aligning our actions with who we are becoming.

Attentional bias means we typically pay more attention to what reinforces our fears, our beliefs, and our assumptions than what disrupts them. Once we've made up our mind about something, we're going to pay attention to signals that confirm what we believe and not what could prove us wrong.

Remember, these cognitive biases are not your fault, but they are your responsibility. Self-transcendence requires awareness of the primitive mind so you can choose differently. Søren Kierkegaard wrote, "The unhappy man is always absent from himself, never present to himself."[24] If you continue to allow your cognitive biases to simplify your thinking, you will be absent from yourself and ultimately unhappy with your life.

We think that by planning for the future, we can maintain control of our lives. We want to believe we can create our future outcomes and be in charge of what happens when, in fact, we're not. And again, it's a fine line. I'm not saying we shouldn't make plans. But we have to be aware of our own tendencies toward hubris.

REFLECTION PAUSE

Presence can be painful because it reveals what we've been avoiding, but it's also the only place we can reclaim anything. We have to stay in the present in order to take back our choice.

◉ AWAKEN

- When did you last go through the motions in a moment that mattered?
- What recent interaction did you rush past that deserved your full presence?

⚲ REMEMBER

- Distraction is drift, and drift is the unconscious accumulation of misaligned choices.
- Presence is the opposite of drift and distraction. Presence is a choice. Presence is participation.

> **← RETURN**

- Who paid for your distraction even if you meant well?
- What moments slipped through your hands because you were chasing something more important?

PRESENCE AND INTEROCEPTION

Before going on, let's revisit interoception because the body is always in the present. The body doesn't plan, rationalize, or regret. It reacts, responds, and remembers. Maurice Merleau-Ponty reminds us that "our own body is in the world as the heart is in the organism: it keeps the visible spectacle constantly alive, it breathes life into it and sustains it inwardly, and with it forms a system."[25] Our body is not in the world like an object. It's our way of being in the world.

Our experiences are not passive. Our sensations, our movements, and our perceptions are not observations of the world. They're how the world becomes meaningful to us. We are not separate from the world around us. We're part of a dynamic, reciprocal flow that creates a system of meaning.

Presence is our only access point to reality, and that access happens through our bodies. We're not observing life from the outside. It's pulsing inside us, and we're pulsing inside that environment. Our body doesn't report the truth. It is the truth. We don't need to *think* our way back to the moment. We need to *feel* our way back in. Our bodies are how we return again and again.

Presence isn't about control; it's about return. Presence through the body is how we begin to transcend thought and rejoin lived reality.

THIS MOMENT WILL NOT COME AGAIN

Do you notice what your body is trying to tell you? Most people I work with don't—not because they don't care but because they've grown used to feeling *off*. Chronic stress from work, life, and everything in between becomes the new normal. They ignore meals, skip rest, and power through. Their sympathetic nervous system stays elevated, but it's so constant that they stop recognizing it as a signal. It's not that they're fine; it's that they've forgotten what fine feels like.

Take a moment. Notice your breath without trying to fix it. Feel your feet inside your shoes. Sense your body weight in the chair. Simply *be*. Ask yourself what your body is telling you.

- What sensations have I been overriding all day?
- What would my body say I want most if I stopped chasing what I want now?
- Where in my body do I feel tension, and when do I feel my body relax?

MORTALITY, MEANING, AND PRESENCE

The focus of this chapter is that this moment will not come again. That's not sentimentality. Time is nonrefundable. American psychologist Irvin Yalom said, "Death and life are interdependent: though the physicality of death destroys us, the idea of death saves us."[26] Existential presence is sharpened by our mortality, the gateway to meaning beyond ego. Death is what gives life meaning.

The reason we're so consumed with planning, strategizing, and forecasting is because there's an underlying assumption. When we feel compelled to make one-, three-, five-, or ten-year plans, the underlying assumption is that we'll be alive to see those plans come to fruition. In essence, we're trying to delay our death by making plans, not that we consciously think about it that way.

Self-transcendence is not about denying death. It's about living with death beside you. When you can clearly see that an end is coming at some point, you will make different choices in the moment. If this were the last thing you could choose, would you choose the same way?

That's reinforced by questions like these:

- What would I say if I knew this was the last time I'd see this person?
- What would I stop waiting to do if I knew I was almost out of time?
- What would change if I lived for what I want most, not for what comforts me now?

Again, I want to reiterate that no one can live like this 100 percent of the time. We have to choose. We have to decide what matters most and then recognize our mortality. If we understand that we're not promised tomorrow, then we can ask if our actions are aligned with what matters most to us. That's what we have to answer for ourselves.

Yes, it's heavy, but it's also true. We have to stand in our choice. That's it. Impermanence isn't the enemy. It's the doorway that brings urgency back into the room. I'm at a point in life where there is clearly more behind me than ahead. But that's not something I fear. It's a sharpening. Death, after all, is the great clarifier. It strips away illusion. It reminds me that every moment I still have is a moment I must meet with intention.

Knowing that certain things will not happen again in my lifetime, my choices become easier. I can say no a lot more clearly and with little remorse because certain things just don't matter anymore. To have that clarity, we have to identify what matters most. Then we can evaluate everything in that context.

Presence is not an achievement. It's a discipline, a moment-by-moment decision to return to what you want most. That's your anchor and your compass. With that firmly in mind, you can evaluate and choose. You can make choices that don't align with that as long as you're consciously making that choice and willing to deal with the consequences.

There's no judgment involved in any of this. It's just the reality that you must choose, recognizing and accepting that there is a choice. Use the Judgment to Curiosity Spectrum as a mirror to determine where you are right now. If you're sitting in Condemnation or Critique, you may be judging yourself and feel shame that what you're doing is wrong. If you're on the Wonder, Curiosity, or Inquiry side, you will likely ask yourself, "What's really here right now?" There's a very different emotional response, depending on where you are positioned.

Vietnamese monk and peace activist Thich Nhat Hanh said, "The present moment is filled with joy and happiness. If you are attentive, you will see it."[27] But we also have to leave room for the other side of life. If we are attentive and present, there will be grief, longing, anxiety, and sadness. That's the truth. And truth is the only foundation for evolution.

We have to have a profound relationship with reality because that's the beginning of self-transcendence, not as a sort of spiritual bypassing but as a radical engagement with what's real—what's here and now. What's real is the only place you choose what you want most.

We have to quit lying to ourselves, imagining the world as we'd like it and making decisions based on that. We need to make decisions based on the world as it is, as we experience it, and as we live it, without judgment.

RETURN FROM THE DRIFT

There's freedom and relief in mastering this approach, that the world is as it is, regardless of what we want. We can make moment-to-moment choices about what we're going to do in a world that's outside our control because the world has always been and always will be out of our control. That's the humility we have to embrace if we want to make meaningful strides toward what matters most to us.

👁 AWAKEN

- What are you postponing that costs you every day?
- What will you regret missing now while you are chasing the future later?

📍 REMEMBER

- Stop pretending you're waiting for clarity.
- Pay attention to what you're doing, because it matters.

↩ RETURN

- If this was it—no next time, no redo—what would you change right now?
- Who are you failing to show up for by staying half-present?

Presence is not the end of the journey. It's the transcendent beginning. And the compass that guides that beginning is not urgency or habit; it's clarity on what we want most.

In the next section, we will transition from Exploration to Experimentation. That is the line between knowing and doing, and it won't cross itself.

So far we've been exploring. We've faced what's been running us. We've interrupted the autopilot long enough to notice the drift, and we've remembered what we want most.

Now comes the real work—not building a perfect plan but stepping into the unknown. We're not waiting to feel ready but returning to our life with new eyes. We're not proving anything but experimenting with everything.

The next phase isn't about certainty. It's about movement. We're not meant to get it right. We're meant to get in the arena. This is the edge of becoming. We need to step in and experiment.

PART II
EXPERIMENT
(WITH COURAGE)

CHAPTER 4

YOU CAN'T THINK YOUR WAY INTO A NEW SELF

You must do the thing you think you cannot do.

ELEANOR ROOSEVELT

Imagine you are planning a vacation. You pack your bags. You make your reservations. Everything is in the car ready to go.

But instead of getting in the car and heading out, you go inside, shut the door, sit down on the couch, and think, "What a great trip!"

Seems pointless, right? No one would do all the prep work, not actually take the trip, and think they'd been on vacation. Planning and thinking will only get you so far. Eventually, you have to act.

THE RECURRENCE EFFECT

In the rhythm of recurrence, you have done the work of Exploring. You've experienced drifting away from what you want most. You've considered the stories you've inherited that may or may not still serve you. And you've begun to accept the impermanence of life and the need to be present as a portal to self-transcendence.

If you're honest with yourself, you're probably feeling uncomfortable right now. That's because you're standing at the threshold of true evolution. You're encountering the tension between where you are and where you long to be. There's no resolution—not yet. But don't rush to escape it.

This discomfort isn't a flaw in the system; it's the invitation. Interoception—your ability to feel what's happening within—is how you learn to stay, not to fix and not to flee but to listen. We're so conditioned to seek relief that we forget that transformation often begins in the body before the mind catches up. Let the tension do its work. Stay long enough to feel what ease would never ask you to face.

This is the first honest moment where you recognize that being aware of the drift, thinking about presence, and acknowledging your desire to change are not enough. It's time to act; it's time to Experiment.

This chapter asks one main question: Will you act even if there's no guarantee your action will work?

That is really the hinge point for recurrence because that is where most of us stop. We'll think about it. We'll talk about it. We'll read about it. We'll contemplate it. We'll do all those things, but we won't take action.

It's not because we're lazy, but we've been conditioned to try to *think* our way into becoming. We want certainty and clarity before we're willing to do anything. We want to plan. We want a guarantee, some promise of return on investment. But that's just not the way the world works.

YOU CAN'T THINK YOUR WAY INTO A NEW SELF

Because we've been conditioned to focus on our brains, we tell ourselves, "I'm going to think this through, and once I get it figured out, I'll take action." But the fact is that we must fight that urge and take action first.

Here's the brutal truth: You will not become different by *understanding;* you will only become different by *doing.*

We must stop pretending that understanding is the same as becoming. I know we've been trained throughout our lives to collect insights like we're building some internal library of transformational quotes, books, podcasts, and concepts that give us a feeling of growth. But most of the time we're not evolving.

We're hiding behind our "knowledge," and it's perfectly disguised procrastination. We won't admit it, but we're not creating anything. We're consuming. We soothe ourselves by thinking like this:

I just need to think this through.
I just need to read another book.
I want to watch this video.
I'm still working on it, but it is just not there yet.

We have all these excuses, but none of them are action. And none of these assurances are really true because we're actually using them to avoid making decisions. Real change doesn't happen in our heads; it happens in our bodies. It happens in decision. It happens in friction. It happens when we're uncomfortable.

Spanish philosopher José Ortega y Gasset wrote, "Life is fired at us point blank."[28] Life isn't offered, delivered, discussed, or read about. It's fired at you. And you're standing there whether you like it or not, right in its path.

If you're waiting for *the* right moment, hoping for clarity before you act, then you've already missed ten chances. Clarity isn't the precondition for movement. Clarity is what you earn after you've moved. You don't find truth by preparing. You find it by showing up in your own life and taking hits.

Don't confuse direction with control. Action is not about destination. It's about direction. It's about moving. It's about committing to a direction, moving, and learning as you go.

The reason that feels awkward or counterintuitive is because we think we get inspired to do things by thinking about them. But our brains are wired to reward us with dopamine only when we *do* things. Dopamine is the neurochemical pursuit. When the brain recognizes that we're in some kind of important action, it dumps dopamine to keep us going.[29]

You will never get dopamine from thinking. You get it from *doing*. You have to act before the dopamine hits. You can't just sit on the sidelines of your own evolution reading the playbook while you imagine action. Being on the sidelines reading the playbook is not the same as being in the game. You have to stop hiding behind thinking and knowing.

Thinking is not doing.

You cannot think your way into a new self. You have to act, try, risk, sweat, and bleed. That's the price of growth. It always has been, and it always will be.

THE GRATITUDE * CHALLENGE GRID

In the next three chapters, we will focus on the second "E" of the Explore, Experiment, Evaluate, and Edit rhythm. Like the Judgment to Curiosity Spectrum that we used in the last section, we have a new mirror to use as we begin to Experiment. The Gratitude × Challenge Grid is a mirror for where you're living and who you're becoming. The grid reveals the invisible architecture of your daily experience. It doesn't label you. It locates you. And once you know where you are, you can decide what you're willing to move toward. *Where* you are isn't *who* you are—but it might become that if you choose to stay there.

The Gratitude × Challenge Grid has high challenge and low challenge on one axis and high gratitude and low gratitude on the other, forming four quadrants: The Cave, the Nest, the Furnace, and the Forge.

This grid wasn't born in some kind of theory. It came out of my real-world experience of working over the last decade with people who were stuck, exhausted, and fading out. It's not because they didn't care anymore. Generally, they cared almost too much at times. The problem was that they didn't know where they were positioned and what being there was costing them.

THE RECURRENCE EFFECT

This grid is really about how you are moving through the world. You don't think your way into those quadrants. You *live* them in your posture, your habits, your breath, and your choices. These are the questions to ask: Where am I now? Where am I willing to move to?

The point isn't to arrive somewhere. It's to return again and again. That isn't a test. It's a mirror that reflects where you are. Where you land on the grid isn't about how you feel. It's about how you show up. It isn't a tool for comfort. It's a mirror for truth. These questions aren't meant to reassure you; they're meant to reveal you.

THE CAVE

As we discuss the quadrants on the Gratitude × Challenge Grid, we'll start at the bottom and work our way up. Starting with where we have low challenge and low gratitude, the bottom left quadrant is the Cave—the illusion of safety and the absence of becoming.

In the Cave, you've retreated, maybe without meaning to. Life feels dull, distant, and gray. You don't feel gratitude. There's no challenge, no perspective, and no pull toward something greater.

You're conserving energy but losing time. You might not even feel stuck—just gone. You've gone silent, not to reflect but to disappear. You mistake avoidance for rest. You're telling yourself you're waiting, but really, you're hiding.

The longer you stay here, the harder it is to come out.

Consider what keeps you here in the Cave:

- What am I protecting by disappearing?
- What emotion have I been avoiding at all costs?
- If nothing changes, what will this cost me in a year?

YOU CAN'T THINK YOUR WAY INTO A NEW SELF

THE NEST

The next quadrant on the lower right is low in challenge, high in gratitude. The Nest is safe, steady, but slowly shrinking. This is comfort with a soft edge. You're thankful, content, and grounded, but you're not growing. You've found your rhythm, but maybe you've stopped risking.

The Nest can be a state of recovery or resignation. You're stable but maybe too still. You're warm, but something inside you is cooling. You're not in danger, but you're also not evolving. What feels like peace may actually be pause, or it might be paralysis.

Ask yourself what may be keeping you in the Nest.

- What challenge am I avoiding in the name of peace?
- What discomfort do I keep deferring until "later"?
- What might happen if I let gratitude fuel courage—not comfort?

THE FURNACE

In the upper left quadrant is the Furnace—high challenge with low gratitude. The Furnace is effort without meaning and fire without purpose. Here, you're grinding, enduring, and proving—but for what?

You took on the challenge—maybe because you had to, maybe because you thought you should—but without gratitude, it corrodes you. You're surviving the heat, but it's not refining you. You wake up dreading the day. You confuse exhaustion with achievement. You've lost the why behind the work.

You're pushing hard but disappearing in the process.

Take a moment to consider what's keeping you in the Furnace.

- What am I proving—and to whom?
- When did I stop being grateful for what I get to do?
- What would it cost me to step out of the fire, even for a moment?

THE FORGE

The last quadrant is in the upper right, which is high challenge with high gratitude. The Forge is where transformation lives. It is where becoming begins. You've chosen challenge—not to suffer but to grow with intention. Gratitude keeps you grounded.

The friction hurts, but it clarifies. You're not waiting to feel ready. You're acting into being. The work is hard, but it's worth it. Your body is tired, but your soul is steady. You're stretched, not broken. You're building integrity, not just endurance.

You're not burning out. You're burning through.

Ask yourself what keeps you in the Forge.

- What keeps me coming back here, even when it's hard?
- What am I willing to sacrifice to keep becoming?
- Who am I becoming when no one's watching?

As you reflect on these questions and discover where you currently find yourself on the grid, remember that you don't *think* your way into these quadrants. You have to *live* them. Maurice Merleau-Ponty wrote, "The body is our general medium for having a world."[30] It's in your posture, and by that I mean how you're stepping into the world—your habits, your breath, your choices.

The grid is a mirror, not a map. Locate yourself. Own it. Then move . . . if you want to.

Where you are isn't wrong, but staying there unconsciously might be. Remember, this isn't about labeling yourself. It's about telling the truth and choosing what comes next. Use the grid to locate yourself, name what's keeping you in that place, and commit to the shift you're done postponing.

REFLECTION PAUSE

This grid doesn't ask you to *fix* yourself. It asks you to *face* yourself. Where you stand today doesn't define you, but it does invite you. And the only quadrant where real transformation happens is the Forge. But no one lives in the Forge full-time. The work is not to stay there; it's to return to it. Use these prompts to find your footing. Don't overthink. Don't justify. Just answer.

👁 AWAKEN

- When was the last time I felt deeply challenged and deeply grateful at the same time?
- What story am I using to avoid friction right now?

📍 REMEMBER

- Each quadrant has its own seduction, its own lie, and its own logic. Use the questions to unearth yours.
- The version of me I want most doesn't exist in theory. It waits on the other side of a decision I've been delaying.

THE RECURRENCE EFFECT

← RETURN

- What's one act of courageous gratitude I can take this week?
- What's one tension I've been labeling as danger that's actually feedback?

ACTING WITHOUT A NET

It's time to act, even if you don't feel ready. Everybody wants to wait until they're ready, but the reality is that you never do anything meaningful when you're ready. That applies at work, at home, and in your personal life because you're never truly ready. If you wait until you're ready, it's often too late. And honestly, if you think you're ready, you're still probably not.

Here's where things get real. This is the turning point between knowing what you want and being willing to risk who you've been in order to become who you want to be. So again, you never really feel ready. There will never be a net. At some point, you either take that leap of faith or you don't. There's no other way to do it.

Freedom doesn't feel very liberating at first. It feels like vertigo. You feel destabilized because now you're fully accountable for your actions. Do you remember how you felt when you first went out on your own as an adult? You started making decisions—finding a place to live and buying clothes and furniture.

Suddenly you realize, *Oh shoot! I have to pay for all this stuff. I need a job. I need insurance. I have to have all these things.* You begin to wonder why you were in a hurry to grow up and become an adult.

Søren Kierkegaard wrote, "Anxiety is the dizziness of freedom."[31] It's normal to feel unsettled, dizzy, anxious, and even queasy. Those feelings are the signal that you're finally facing your life without a script. You're not confused; you're awake. Jean-Paul Sartre called the feeling nausea.[32] It is nauseating to realize that it's all on you.

To have that life you want, you have to create it without knowing if it will work. You have to initiate the actions that you believe will create the change you crave without knowing if it will work. There are no guarantees. Freedom doesn't always feel liberating.

Simone de Beauvoir said, "To will oneself moral and to will oneself free are one and the same decision."[33] This is the moment when we have to stop outsourcing our lives. We have to realize that freedom isn't the absence of limits; it's the presence of alignment. De Beauvoir dares us to show we're free by how we live, how we lead, and how we carry the weight of that freedom.

Choose what's right, not what's easy. Be an example to other people. Embody your philosophy. You don't have to tell anybody what you believe if you embody it.

Freedom is meaningless if you don't pair it with integrity. To choose your path is also to choose your own impact. You're free to act but also responsible for what your action creates. Freedom without morality is ego, and morality without freedom is obedience.

Everybody gets wound up about freedom, about wanting to be free to do certain things and not have their freedoms restricted. The problem is that we fail to understand the repercussions of our freedom. Our actions send out ripples. We are responsible for those ripples. We can't just say, "Well, that wasn't what I intended."

I told my kids when they were all young adults that everybody always talks about being able to make their own decisions. And they're entirely correct. You are free to make your own decisions—and also free to accept the responsibilities and implications that come with those decisions.

THE RECURRENCE EFFECT

What you're stepping into is not just risk. It's not about the adrenaline rush. It is about being aligned with what matters most because when your decisions are based on what you want most, you're willing to suffer those consequences. As Friedrich Nietzsche said, "If we have our own why in life, we shall get along with almost any how."[34] That is what becoming looks like.

Becoming involves grounded decisions that cost you something. Your values, your mission, and your beliefs—none of those work until they cost you something.

There's no hack. There's no easy way. There's no easy button. As Mother Teresa said, "There are no great things, only small things done with great love." This isn't about grand gestures or shortcuts to success. That's where we get out of whack because everybody wants something instantaneous.

We want immediate transformation, but it just doesn't work that way. Quick and easy change is not sustainable. And what we're after here is *sustainable* evolution.

To act with freedom is to own your impact. To become is to commit to alignment, not just with your desires but with your values. You're not here to get it right. There is no right. You're here to risk becoming. It is a continual effort. That's why the mantra of the Relentless Few is that "we're done when we're dead"—hopefully.

THE RITUALS OF BECOMING

You don't become new by making a declaration. Words without action are meaningless. Michael Scott in *The Office* stated, "I declare bankruptcy!" But you can't just make a statement and act like the work is done.[35] That's what we're tempted to do. We think we're going to make a declaration and just be done.

YOU CAN'T THINK YOUR WAY INTO A NEW SELF

We confuse saying something with doing it, and neuroscience shows why. When we declare a goal or share a plan, the brain releases dopamine, giving us a hit of satisfaction as if we've already taken action. But that's the danger: The reward comes prematurely.

We *feel* progress without making any. The brain begins to map the outcome, and we start behaving as though we've already done the work when all we've actually done is talk about it. It's a cognitive loop—the more we say it, the more we believe we're living it. But we're not. Until action interrupts the loop, we're just rehearsing a future we haven't earned.

You become new by building rituals—lived, repeated, sacred actions that reinforce who you're choosing to become. Rituals are done not once, not as a breakthrough, but daily, quietly, and relentlessly. There are no peak moments. Nobody's applauding. There's no dopamine hit—just repetition, recalibration, and return.

If the Forge is fire, then ritual is how you stand in it. Rituals aren't about control. They're about attention, not to your plan but to your posture—how you walk through the world. They're not about your outcomes but your orientation. The Forge is direction, not destination.

You have to attend to those rituals, figure out what they are, and be relentless. Drift doesn't announce itself. It doesn't knock on the door. It doesn't scream. It whispers. It delays. It soothes. It says, "Hey, you can skip this ritual once. It won't matter."

By the time you realize it, you've drifted far from who you said you were becoming. It's strategic drift. You have a strategy, but you're just slowly drifting away through a series of micro-decisions you make over time—a micro-decision here and a micro-decision there. It wasn't a sudden change of direction. You made a bunch of what you thought were insignificant decisions and yet woke up one day pointed in an entirely different direction. That's what happens to all of us if we're not paying attention, if we're not returning. We are not just drifting. We are adrift.

Ritual is how you remember who you are when everything around you wants to forget. Rituals are sacred. You can't *not* do them, right? It's like brushing your teeth. About once every other week, I'll be tired and go to bed without brushing my teeth. Thirty seconds after lying down, I realize I didn't brush my teeth. So I get out of bed, go into the bathroom, and brush my teeth because it pulls me. I can't *not* do it.

That to me is ritual, which is more than habit. Habit is not thinking. Ritual is deep thinking in my mind. Ritual is how I stabilize my identity through friction. It's how I say what needs to be said, even when it's messy and especially when it's inconvenient or uncomfortable. It's waking up early to do the thing no one sees, knowing it may not be the *thing* that matters but the *fact* that I am doing it that does.

Those rituals aren't performances to be talked about and expanded upon. They're things that we do in the quiet. It's choosing stillness when distraction would be easier. It's not getting on your phone and scrolling but doing meaningful work—creating something or being attentive to some*one* instead of some*thing*, and returning to gratitude.

When bitterness tempts you to act like a victim and say, "Well, what else could I do? What else could I possibly have done? I didn't have any choice." That's bad faith, as Sartre called it.[36]

Picking up the weight of your own agency and maintaining authorship of your story isn't a strategy. It's a signal. It tells the truth about what matters and, more importantly, about who's willing to act like it does. That is the philosophical spine of ritual.

Albert Camus wrote, "Real generosity towards the future lies in giving all to the present."[37]

His point is powerful because it gives a different view of why the present is so important. We talk about the present like it's an end in and of itself. In meditation, we talk about being present and grounded. But we often don't talk about the present as a *means* to an end.

Being present doesn't get you anything. The point is being present *for* something. When you're fully attentive in the present, you make a better future for yourself.

The present is the only point of power. Many people want to fantasize about the future version of themselves and what they can accomplish. They imagine who they'll be when things settle down, when things make sense, and when the conditions are right. But Camus disagrees with that.

You don't create a meaningful future by imagining it. Visualization without embodiment is a fantasy. The future is forged in the unnoticed moments—the mundane, the repetitive, the ones that feel too small to matter, but they do because those moments shape you. These are not the breakthroughs, not the retreats, not the grand declarations, but the quiet, daily return to what's necessary. That's where the real work happens. That's what builds a future, and that's what generosity to your future self actually looks like.

In practice, generosity looks like showing up before you're ready, acting before you're sure, or moving without knowing where you'll end up. Those are the ways that you can, in Camus' words, give real generosity toward the future because the future is not some abstract reward for your preparation. The future is the cumulative effect of what you return to again and again.

THE RECURRENCE EFFECT

Ritual is resistance. Ritual is rebellion. Ritual is how you revolt against your own drift because it's what returns you. Those rituals aren't glamorous. Ritual is how you return, not to perfection and not to performance but to the Forge where you want to be. You want to be in the place where high gratitude and high challenge collide.

When drift is pulling you, ask yourself, "What's one small embodied act I can do today that reconnects me to who I said I was becoming? Where am I most tempted to disengage? What ritual would anchor me instead of numb me?"

When you feel lost, ask, "What's the first thing I abandon when I start to spiral?"

Think about it. We all have patterns.

What rhythm, no matter how small, reminds you that you're still in the work now when nobody's watching?

A quiet ritual is just for you, a private personal declaration that you're still showing up. Nobody else needs to see it or understand it. What does integrity look like in the absence of an audience? This is a big one. You don't have to post about it. You don't have to take a picture of it. You don't have to tell anybody about it.

Integrity is asking, "What am I doing in the quiet time now when I'm waiting for clarity? What would it look like to act intentionally but before I feel ready? What's the next repetition, not the next big revelation?"

Again, you don't need more novel ideas. You need to return to the action.

When you need to return to the Forge, consider this: "What do I *not* want to do today that I know I *must* do?"

Simple, repeated practice stokes that fire—not for performance but for presence.

YOU CAN'T THINK YOUR WAY INTO A NEW SELF

DISCOMFORT IS THE DOOR

This is the point where most people want to turn around. The tension, the unease, the discomfort leads many to make a quick U-turn. This is not just the surface kind of discomfort. It's not an inconvenience or friction in your schedule.

This is the existential kind of discomfort, the kind that shows up when you stop performing. It's the one that visits you in silence when no one else is around or confronts you when you realize what you're doing isn't working anymore. And remember, there's no script to get past that discomfort.

From an evolutionary perspective, discomfort was a signal—a warning system to keep us alive. Pain meant danger. Fatigue meant rest. Fear meant "Run!" For much of human history, that wiring served us well. But in the modern world, that same wiring misfires.

We've advanced to a point where we rarely face true threats, yet we still treat any discomfort—emotional, physical, or psychological—as a problem to eliminate. We've come to believe that if something feels uncomfortable, it must be wrong. But evolution didn't prepare us for growth. It prepared us for survival. That's the trap. The very mechanisms that once protected us now insulate us from the discomfort we *need* in order to evolve.

Existential discomfort, Sartre's nausea, is essential for evolution. Feeling that doesn't mean you're broken. If you're uncomfortable in this tension, you didn't fail. If it's uncomfortable, you shouldn't abort the mission and retreat to something familiar. That's not becoming; that's the Nest.

Evolution is like a J-curve. To go up, to get to where you want to be, you have to go down into the valley of despair and discomfort. It doesn't feel good because you're trying something different. It's new and unfamiliar. And it's not going to work perfectly every time.

Discomfort lives in the valleys, and you can't avoid it by trying to go from mountaintop to mountaintop. You have to go down into the valley first.

That discomfort is not a sign of failure. It's actually the threshold to becoming, so the best thing you can do is embrace it. I'm not saying you need to be comfortable with being uncomfortable. That's not the point. I don't think we should ever be comfortable with discomfort. But we need to be able to sit with it, live with it, and learn from it.

The goal isn't comfort. It's about recognizing discomfort for the value it brings because once you feel that discomfort, you're doing the work of becoming. You're doing it right. If it feels uncomfortable, the discomfort is proof that you've stopped watching your life and are going to start embodying it.

Discomfort is how your nervous system tells the truth. When your ego wants to lie to you and take you back to "safety," that's when your body's response tells you you're on the right track. That often looks like this:

- The anxiety that appears when you finally tell the truth, when you feel compelled to share something with somebody.
- The tension in your chest when you say what needs to be said and the room goes completely silent.
- That moment when you think, *Oh shoot! Now what's going to happen?*
- The fear of being misunderstood but going ahead and saying it anyway.

YOU CAN'T THINK YOUR WAY INTO A NEW SELF

- The trembling when you realize this next act matters and there's no guarantee it will be received well, but you're willing to step out there.

These are not signs that something has gone wrong. They're evidence that you're awake. It's right there in this brutal, beautiful moment that there's power. Swedish author Pär Lagerkvist wrote in his book, "The Dwarf" that "Human beings like the see themselves reflected in clouded mirrors." , .

We're not going to romanticize this. Lagerkvist wasn't being poetic — he was being precise. He was naming our tendency to blur what's real so we can avoid the sharp edges of truth.

We'd rather look through fog than face the reflection staring back. We distort the image just enough to stay comfortable, to keep our illusions intact. But clarity always demands a cost — and that cost is our comfort.

Truths don't hide behind metaphors. You're going to die. No one else can live your life. There's no book, no podcast, no framework that can do the work for you. You are the author of your own becoming, and authorship isn't safe. It requires responsibility, courage, and the willingness to stand unguarded before what's true.

Meaning isn't found in the haze. It's forged when you wipe the mirror clean — when you see yourself as you are, not as you wish to be. And that moment of clarity doesn't comfort you. It confronts you. It strips away every excuse and leaves you with one question that matters:

Now that you can finally see — what will you do?

Most people opt out here, not because they don't care but because they care a lot. They want to change, but they don't want to feel the truth of what they already know. Deep down inside,

THE RECURRENCE EFFECT

each and every one of us knows this. We want to anesthetize ourselves with money, pleasure, or whatever so we don't have to think about these things and feel the discomfort.

But this is where the Relentless Few live. They don't chase comfort. They chase clarity. They earn it by walking through discomfort—without a map, without a guarantee.

In the relentless view, we don't sugarcoat the struggle. We're not pretending discomfort is just a phase to push through or a stage to overcome. We stay with it because we know that's where becoming happens.

Discomfort isn't an obstacle; it's the Forge itself. When we feel discomfort, that's when we're in the Forge—high gratitude and high challenge. The Forge is discomfort realized. The work isn't to minimize it; the work is to build the capacity to hold it, to stand with it, to sit with it and not flinch, and to be okay with it.

We all need to learn how to sit with discomfort because you don't become the next version of yourself by *thinking* about it. As we've said before, you become it when you stop bargaining with your pain and start building with it. We're not trying to avoid pain or get out of the pain we're currently in. We're going to use it as the building block for becoming.

Discomfort is not dysfunction. It's your life pushing back, asking you if you're willing to do more than understand. It's that tension between the current you and the one that's trying to emerge.

You can't remain what you are and become what you're going to be. You can't go around it. You can't talk your way through it. You have to go through it. You have to move and take action.

On the other side is not ease, not resolution, and not a reward. On the other side, you find *you*—stripped, shaped, and still standing—ready to begin again.

That's what the Relentless Few return to—not certainty, not security, but the willingness to feel all of it and keep going anyway, to be 100 percent in the world and feel it all.

RETURN FROM THE DRIFT

Remember, this isn't merely reflection. This is accountability. This isn't about winning or losing. It's about moving forward. You don't need another insight. You need a moment of defiance to choose, move, and return.

👁 AWAKEN

- Where am I labeling discomfort as dysfunction?
- Where have I been calling fear "timing" or avoidance "strategy"?

📍 REMEMBER

- Discomfort isn't evidence that I'm broken.
- Discomfort is the invitation I've been waiting to reject.

↩ RETURN

- What's the friction I'm willing to walk into—not because I'll win but because it's mine to face?

THE RECURRENCE EFFECT

This is the edge of becoming. This isn't the climax; it's the ignition point. You've seen what's shaped you. You've told the truth about where you are. Now comes the cost of who you could become.

As you read in the beginning of this chapter, Eleanor Roosevelt said, "You must do the thing you think you cannot do."[38] You do this thing not because you're fearless but because you're finally done waiting. This chapter isn't about action that works. It's about action that wakes you up.

The door's open.

Discomfort is waiting.

Step in.

Welcome to the Forge.

CHAPTER 5

THE BIOLOGY OF BECOMING

To be what we are, and to become what we are capable of becoming, is the only end of life.

ROBERT LOUIS STEVENSON

In *The Matrix*, when Neo wakes up for the first time in the real world, the quiet stillness sharply contrasts with the adrenaline-fueled action of the previous scenes. Neo sees himself as he really is, not his Matrix-generated self-image. He's clearly disconcerted. You can see the hint of doubt creeping into his eyes as he wonders what the hell he just did.[39]

Maybe you feel the same right now. In the previous chapter, you took that leap of faith into becoming. Now we're moving

THE RECURRENCE EFFECT

from the adrenaline of acting into the aftermath. Like Neo, everything in your body is starting to question what you've done.

The aftermath—the landing—isn't about mindset. It's not about reframing the story, mental toughness, or clarity. It's about what happens to your body and your nervous system when you stop performing and start becoming. That's where the discomfort gets very real, not theoretically but physically. That is where your brain's storylines collide with your body's alarms—the shallow breath, the racing heart, the clench in your gut.

We're not describing fear. We're describing the embodied consequence of our actions. Because you've just crossed that threshold, acting without a guarantee, you're now in a disorienting place where your old identity doesn't fit anymore. But your new one isn't fully present yet either.

The feeling is not just uncertainty. It's full exposure, and exposure lives in the body. Austrian-Israeli philosopher Martin Buber wrote, "All real living is meeting."[40] I want you to just sit with that for a moment.

Real living is not planning. It's not rehearsal. It's not downloading another playbook or reflecting one more time. Living is about a real meeting. Martin Buber's point is that real transformation doesn't happen in isolation but in the encounter in the moment. When you show up fully, you drop the performance and meet reality, another person, or yourself without a buffer of control.

That's where you are now. You're not just thinking about life anymore. You're in it. You've lost the safety of the bleachers. You're on the field—bruised, exposed, fully visible, without a script—so of course your body responds.

When you meet something real, when you encounter that thing that matters, your body's response is not neutral. It shakes you. It stirs you. Sometimes it breaks you wide open, and that's not dysfunction. That's the biology of becoming.

The next step is reorienting yourself. You're not broken. You're becoming. Your body's response isn't a glitch. It's the echo of your new self trying to stabilize. That is the Experiment part of the 4E rhythm.

It is also the most visceral element. It's no longer about exploring ideas or outcomes. This is the movement. This is action. This is exposure.

These actions reside distinctly in the body, and the body doesn't lie. Feel the cost of being in the work—the sweat, breath, clenching, insomnia, and impulse. We're laying the groundwork for everything that follows. If you do this right, you'll stop asking, "What's wrong with me?" and start asking, "What's this sensation trying to teach me?"

Discomfort becomes orientation. That's the point. This is the moment in the arc when you know you're not here to feel better. You're here to stay awake. Keep moving and don't flinch from what you're feeling.

REVISITING THE GRATITUDE × CHALLENGE GRID

Going back to the Gratitude × Challenge Grid, we're going to use it to help figure out where we've landed. In the previous chapter, we introduced the grid as a mirror, and now we're crawling inside it. We want to embody it.

We're shifting our experience with the grid from something cognitive to something cellular. We're not contemplating what quadrant we're in but we're asking, "What is my body living right now?" In this exercise, the grid is more of a topographical map of the self under pressure.

THE RECURRENCE EFFECT

As you use the Gratitude × Challenge Grid to figure out where you've landed, pay attention to your body's physical cues and the sensory input you're getting.

THE FURNACE

Let's start with the Furnace. That's where most people typically sit, in the high-challenge, low-gratitude quadrant. There you're grinding and pushing, maybe even doing some brave things, but you're bitter. You're exhausted. You feel alone in your work. You're resenting the very things you used to love. In the Furnace, your body feels tight, probably over-caffeinated.

Everything is a struggle. Nothing is enough, and maybe no one knows because on the outside you still look productive. The question is this: "Am I trying to *prove* something or *become* someone?"

That's the dissonance you feel in the Furnace. As you evolve, you're not trying to prove. You're trying to become.

Being in the Furnace might feel like the following scenario: It's Thursday afternoon. You're exhausted. You just told someone the truth. You're not sure what comes next, but for once you don't spin it. You're here. You've stayed. You may feel lost, but you're not. You're in the Furnace.

THE NEST

Next we drop into the Nest—low challenge, high gratitude. We're going from the upper left to the lower right quadrant. The Nest is tricky because on the surface it usually feels good.

You're grateful. You've got space. You're not in crisis. But if you sit still long enough, you'll notice that the hunger kind of goes away. The stretch is missing.

Since you're not stretching, you're actually shrinking in the name of contentment. Here you want to ask, "Have I confused peace with passivity?"

The Nest doesn't always feel bad, but it slowly erodes your edge. You feel it in your calendar, in your posture, and in your slowly lowering standards.

If you've landed in the Nest, you may experience a scenario like this: It's Monday morning. You aren't anxious or rushing to get to work. You sip your coffee as you stroll into your first meeting of the day. You're glad for the peace you feel, but you have no curiosity about where you're headed. You think you're resting, but really you're getting a little too comfortable in the Nest.

THE CAVE

Moving to the bottom left, we arrive at the Cave—low challenge, low gratitude. This is the place of drift. This is disconnection, silence, maybe burnout, and maybe even shame.

But it's not numbness. It's avoidance. It's not healing. It's hiding.

There's no shame in landing here. You need to name that ache. Listen for the voice that says, "If I don't care, I can't fail."

That's the Cave. It's cold—not loud, just absent.

When you find yourself in the Cave, it takes effort to name the drift. Imagine it's Friday. You're sitting at your computer watching the clock, waiting for the end of the workday. You don't have plans. You're not excited about anything much. You feel distant and alone in the Cave like you're avoiding life.

THE FORGE

Finally, we jump up to the upper right quadrant. That's the Forge—high challenge, high gratitude. The Forge is the only place where true evolution lives. It's where discomfort meets presence. It's certainly not pain-free. It's not easy, but it's aligned.

You don't feel heroic there, but you feel honest. There's fire, but you're facing it. You're not just performing in front of it. You're fully in the Forge.

This is a space where the experiment starts to forge something new, not because it's working yet but because you're staying in it long enough for it to mean something. You aren't dropping out of the discomfort.

Being in the Forge can feel like reaching the end of a 10-mile hike. Your body is still under a lot of stress, but your posture has shifted. You're not bracing yourself anymore. You're breathing through it. It's hard, but there's satisfaction in becoming who you are meant to be.

Wherever you've landed, the key move here is not diagnosis; the goal is to locate yourself in your body, your breath, and your choices. Feel where you live and then ask yourself, "If I'm not where I want to be, am I willing to move?"

We're at the bottom of the J-curve, and we have to keep going. To evolve, we can't go back or jump forward too quickly.

REFLECTION PAUSE

This is where we learn to reinterpret the pain we're feeling. Since this is the most emotionally destabilizing part of the Experiment phase, the temptation is either to try to Evaluate too soon or retreat back into Exploration. This isn't relief. This is reality. You've moved. You're in it; now feel it.

👁 AWAKEN

- Where am I mistaking this discomfort for failure instead of formation?
- What part of me is trying to escape back to clarity?

📍 REMEMBER

- Discomfort isn't dysfunction; it's evidence. I'm no longer pretending.
- The drop I'm in isn't the end. It's the beginning of something that matters.

↩ RETURN

- What small act of courage today keeps me from retreating, not to win but to stay?
- What truth am I willing to face without needing to fix or flee so I can move forward honestly?

DISCOMFORT AS FEEDBACK, NOT FAILURE

Our natural inclination when life gets uncomfortable is to hurry the process and start looking for meaning. At this stage, what we need is capacity. That's what we're trying to build in the Experiment phase.

The work here isn't to figure it all out. The work is to stay

THE RECURRENCE EFFECT

in the discomfort long enough for it to work on you. Don't rush through the Experiment.

You just made the courageous move. You took the step, and now things feel worse. Your confidence is gone. Your clarity is lacking, and your identity is cracking. That's *exactly* what should be happening.

Pain is not a problem. It's feedback. Again, I'm not saying discomfort is good and that you should be comfortable with discomfort. I'm saying discomfort is data. It's a body-level signal that says you're now out of the old pattern.

Discomfort is not a sign that anything's wrong. It's a sign that something is no longer familiar. Those are different things. You're not going backward. You're going deeper.

You may feel like being in the valley of despair is failure, but it's not. This is the fire that's doing the work. You haven't fallen off a cliff. You've descended into the valley of despair. That part of the J-curve feels like regression, but it's actually evolution in progress.

The J-curve is a lived arc. You took a risk. You stepped outside your pattern. You expected freedom, and now you feel foggy, exposed, and unsure. That's how the J-curve is supposed to make you feel.

That drop is natural and expected, even necessary. The mistake most people make is trying to get out of it too early and thinking that discomfort means they've done something wrong.

You need to flip the pain, the doubt, and the silence. That's what the work feels like when you're not numbing or avoiding it. You want to feel this.

Pain isn't the enemy. It's the most honest mirror. We never encounter the world as it is, only as we are. Pain doesn't distort reality. It *reveals* how we relate to it. We keep looking for insight like it's hiding in a theory. But sometimes it's already happening in the body—in the breath we hold, in the silence we avoid, in the tension we carry. As Merleau-Ponty put it, "The relation to the world, such as it tirelessly announces itself within us, is not something that analysis might clarify: philosophy can simply place it before our eyes and invite us to take notice."[41] That's what we're doing here—not solving, not explaining, but *noticing*. Real transformation begins when we stop analyzing the fire and start *standing in it*.

Pain is disruptive. It makes you rearrange how you see yourself, your work, and your relationships. It truly does destabilize your identity. That's not dysfunction. That's the dismantling of your false self.

Push through the discomfort and name the signals of pain—societal withdrawal, shame, hypervigilance, tight chest. Notice your internal narrative. When you start asking yourself, "Why did I do this? Did I screw it up? Wasn't it better before?" sit with the feedback and don't run away from it. That is where you begin to learn that pain is not the problem. It's actually a pulse.

The feedback isn't cognitive. It's embodied. I'm not asking you to interpret the discomfort or think about it. You need to feel it fully enough to let it change you. So again, you have to resist the urge to jump to your head. Stay in your body.

The point is to get out of the loop of act, feel discomfort, retreat, explain, and repeat. Instead, shift into act, feel discomfort, stay, listen, and evolve. Your job here is not to solve the discomfort. It's actually to legitimize it as part of the becoming process.

This isn't you falling apart. This is your old identity falling off. It isn't failure. It's exposure. You're not being punished. You're being rewired.

Stay with it. Don't evaluate yet. Here's the challenge: As soon as discomfort shows up, you will be tempted to reflect, evaluate, and say, "Did it work?" But you need to wait. Don't move on before the fire is done changing you. That's how people short-circuit their evolution.

You're not ready to Evaluate yet. You are still in the Experiment phase. Evaluation will come after the smoke has cleared, not when you're still breathing fire. Stay in the Experiment without trying to extract insight from it right away. Truth doesn't arrive in a tidy package. It actually emerges from the wreckage.

The instability you feel right now is purposeful. Discomfort is the doorway into becoming. That's what we're heading to next. Let the fire speak. Let the discomfort mean something. Don't retreat or rush ahead. There is a way to stay present without burning out. Ritual is how you keep from collapsing while standing in the fire.

RITUALS OF CONTAINMENT

You are in the valley of despair. You've acted without guarantees. You're in discomfort, and everything familiar is falling away or no longer working for you.

Here's the thing: You can't think your way through this. You can't evaluate your way out, and you surely can't perform your way out of this. What you need now is containment. Rituals are what allow you to stay in the fire without flinching or collapsing.

Rituals, as we've discussed, are the lived, repeated, sacred actions that reinforce who you are becoming. Rituals aren't an escape from discomfort. They're endurance, but not in the sense of control, discipline, optimization, or structure. That's not how we're using them here. Rituals are a way to stay upright through the discomfort of becoming.

Ritual is what gives form to your presence. When you're in the Forge and everything else feels like it's burning away, ritual allows you to remain inside the fire without being consumed by it. It's not strategy; it's stance.

Rituals stabilize identity. In the absence of clarity, rituals should feel like a return to breath. They're not relief, but they're rhythm. In the Experiment phase, there's no certainty and no outcome, and you're not sure who you are or where you're going. That's where ritual saves you—not by giving you answers but by holding your shape while everything around you feels like chaos.

At that point, you don't need to know what's next. You just need one thing: return to your rituals. That's how you remind yourself who you said you are becoming—not with words but with movement, breath, posture, and repetition.

Rituals are mirrors, not mechanisms. They are signals, not solutions. Every ritual is a declaration, not to others but to yourself to say, "I'm still in it. I still care. I haven't abandoned the work even if no one sees me doing it."

These aren't tactics. They're acts of self-remembrance. When your body wants to dissociate, when your mind wants to narrate, or when your spirit wants to numb, the ritual says, "Stay here. Feel this. You're still in the story."

As you practice your rituals of containment, focus on the following to help you return:

- **BREATH:** When everything is loud, come back to inhale and exhale. It's not meditation; it's just survival. Before you explain yourself, just remember to breathe.

- **MOVEMENT:** Shift your body, walk, stretch, and get into your limbs. Movement reminds you that you're not trapped. When the story is spiraling, move before you believe it.

- **NAMING:** Say what hurts. Write it down, speak it out loud. Don't let it fester. Unnamed language doesn't heal, but naming gives pain a shape.

- **STILLNESS:** Don't reach for your phone. Don't buffer the silence. Let stillness break the momentum of panic. You're not waiting; you're anchoring.

- **BOUNDARIES:** Protect your energy. Don't overexplain. Say no because sometimes containment means stepping back, not giving in.

Each of these is a practice of integrity. In the absence of applause or clarity, these aren't simply healthy habits. They're actually quiet defiance.

Rituals are how you carry your identity through fire. Rituals aren't about doing what's "right." They're about staying true. That is how you remember who you are when you forget everything else. Rituals are how you carry your identity forward through discomfort, through exposure, and through doubt without dropping it in favor of something easy.

This is your anchor point, your foothold inside the Experiment when nothing else feels solid. This is the rhythm of recurrence, the rhythm of return, and the rhythm of presence. Rituals make space for authenticity to emerge.

RETURN FROM THE DRIFT

As you discover where you've landed after your leap of faith, remember what's important. You're still here. This is not an accident; it's a decision. Before going on, be sure you have already returned to yourself in the ritual. Take a moment to sit with your answers to the following questions and thoughts:

👁 AWAKEN

- Where am I still expecting relief?
- Instead of learning how to remain in the Forge, what part of me is whispering, "Just go back. It was safer there"?

📍 REMEMBER

- The fire isn't punishing me. It's purifying what's false.
- This isn't about outcomes. It's about alignment, presence, and defiance.

↩ RETURN

- What is one discomfort I'm willing to carry this week, not to be heroic but to be honest?
- What ritual can I return to when applause is absent and only integrity remains?

You've stopped waiting for clarity. You've stepped into discomfort. You've stayed longer than most would, and now something else starts to happen. The image you used to present to the world—the persona, the certainty, the polish—begins to crack, not because you failed but because you're no longer performing.

You're no longer managing perception. You're no longer explaining. You're no longer adjusting your truth to make others comfortable. When you stop performing, you don't disappear. You arrive raw, real, unfinished, and finally free.

THE RECURRENCE EFFECT

In the next chapter, we'll take off the masks we wear when we're performing. We'll talk about what happens when we stop performing—not just for others but for ourselves.

CHAPTER 6

THE COLLAPSE OF THE MASK

I tore myself away from the safe comfort of certainties through my love for truth—and truth rewarded me.

SIMONE DE BEAUVOIR

You know the dream where you're standing in front of a crowd and then realize you're not wearing any clothes. You feel embarrassed, exposed, and unprotected. In the dream—nightmare, really—you start to panic and try to find something to cover yourself. You don't want anyone to see you that way. It's a relief to wake up and know it was just a dream, although that unsettled feeling lingers.

THE RECURRENCE EFFECT

Dreams like that about being naked in public often stem from our fears about vulnerability, exposure, and embarrassment. We may also be afraid of people seeing or knowing who we really are or what we really want. That same sense of insecurity and nakedness is how we are probably feeling at this stage in the process of becoming.

This is where the mask slips, and not just the surface-level mask we wear in front of others. I'm talking about the mask we wear for *ourselves*—the curated image, the internal performance, that polished version we try to believe is real enough. Like Neo in *The Matrix*, we have a residual self-image made up of how we want to be seen.[42]

What happens when that fabricated self-image collapses? That performance can't hold forever. At some point, you have to drop the mask, not because you're choosing to be authentic but because you're tired. You're simply too tired to keep pretending.

The previous chapter brought you to the edge. You've taken the plunge and acted without a net. You've stayed in the discomfort. You've learned to hold the fire through ritual. Now we see what burned away when the fire kept going—all the parts of you that were never true to begin with. But remember, you haven't arrived yet. You've only just landed, and the fire is still burning.

Now we begin with what's left when your performative self is finally all burned away. It's not because you made some notable declaration but because you couldn't keep holding it up. This is the collapse—not a breakdown but a breakthrough that actually breaks.

Going back to what Martin Heidegger wrote, "Everyone is the other, and no one is himself."[43] That mask you wore wasn't just a lie you told others. It was a life you lived, and maybe it was the only version of you that you believed was worth keeping.

THE COLLAPSE OF THE MASK

At this point, you're not pretending anymore, but you're not entirely clear either. This is what it feels like when you drop from the Forge into the Cave—not as a failure but as a reckoning. The lights are off. The applause has stopped. You're in the dark with your breath and the sound of your own becoming. In truth, you built that mask to survive. The problem isn't survival; it's living.

The mask you wore and your performance weren't just for others. They were also for you. I'm not here to give you a TED Talk about being more authentic. This work isn't about trying to get applause for vulnerability. I want you to see something deeper and much more threatening.

Our most dangerous performances are the ones we convince ourselves are necessary. That high-achieving, self-sufficient, got-it-all-together self wasn't armor against the world. That was a narrative you built to feel worthy, and now it's crumbling. You've stopped performing, but you haven't arrived at some pristine integrated self. You're standing in rubble, whispering to yourself, "If I'm not that, then who the hell am I?"

The collapse of your performative self feels like death. The loss of a performed identity isn't freeing at first. It's disorienting and destabilizing, and it feels like dying because in some ways it is. This is the death of your ego. It's not transcendence at this point. It's just rupture.

What it feels like now is standing in front of the mirror and not recognizing who's looking back. It's like sitting in a room full of people and realizing you don't know what to say when you're not performing. It's like the uncomfortable silence when you stop saying what you think people want to hear and realize that no one is rushing in to applaud you. This is that kind of freeze moment. It's not fight or flight. It's just freeze because there's nothing left to perform and no script for what comes next.

THE RECURRENCE EFFECT

You need to know that your mask wasn't a lie. It was a survival strategy. There is no shame in having worn the mask and performed an identity. It kept you alive. It got you through. It protected the most tender parts of you when you didn't have the capacity to face them directly. But now you see that it's an outdated version of you, and the performance that protected you has started suffocating you.

What once made you strong now restrains you. You've outgrown the act, and now the stage feels too small. You're shedding a skin that no longer fits you. Like a favorite pair of pants that now fit too tightly, those false selves felt comfortable for a long time but not anymore. It's normal to feel a sense of loss as you put them away, but it's time to move on.

When the applause stops, the work begins. The most dangerous part of stopping the performance is that you don't get rewarded. There's no audience for rawness and no standing ovation for your honesty. Sometimes there's just silence. You need to ask yourself, "If no one claps, do I still stay true?" This work is done mostly in the dark where no one sees or applauds. The only way authenticity becomes real is when it costs you something and you stay in it anyway.

When the validation stops and you're left vulnerable and alone on stage, it will feel like withdrawal. You've quit getting high from approval, and you will feel it in your body—the trembling hands, the nausea, the ache of not being recognized. There's no shortcut through it. There's no numbing or quick fix.

As with all the stages of our evolution, we will return to these feelings with every collapse. That is part of the recurrence. The collapse doesn't happen just once but every time you choose truth over performance. Each time it costs a little less, but it will never be free.

THE COLLAPSE OF THE MASK

The performance is over. The mask is gone, but you're still here. You're standing in the open air, exposed and realizing no one's coming to save you. Still, you must resist the urge to pick up the mask again. When you stop chasing clarity and start choosing alignment, the real work begins. If you're still reading, you're ready to move forward.

THE SEDUCTION OF REPERFORMANCE

Even though you've dropped the mask, it hasn't disappeared. Performance waits. The minute the silence gets too loud, the mask offers certainty and comfort. We're drawn to return to the Nest where there is gratitude but no stretch, no fire. It's seductive. It feels restful and comforting, but there's no evolution, no change, and no growth.

Simone de Beauvoir wrote, "One is not born, but rather becomes a woman."[44] She wasn't just talking about gender. She was naming this deeper truth: We are not born into ourselves. We become through friction, not ease. Becoming isn't a moment. It's a war with what makes you comfortable. Just when you've dropped the mask, you'll feel the pull to reach for it again to smooth over the discomfort, to explain and soften your truth until it's palatable for other people again. But every time you do—even in micro-movements—you teach your nervous system that truth is unsafe, that honesty needs editing, and that presence needs permission. And that's how you betray the very self you were becoming.

There is no judgment in figuring out where you are. There is only courage—or the lack of it. The Gratitude × Challenge Grid isn't a test. It's a mirror. It doesn't label you. It simply reflects the truth of your current posture with no reward and no punishment—just orientation. And yet most people avoid it, not because they can't read the map but because they're afraid of what it might reveal.

W. E. B. Du Bois wrote, "There is but one coward on earth, and that is the coward that dare not know."[45] Knowing takes nerve because once you *see* where you are—the Nest, the Furnace, the Cave—you can't unsee it. You either move or settle into stillness. That mask you're holding? It's fear pretending to be wisdom. It tells you that staying quiet is mature, that downshifting is "balance," that not knowing is humility. But really? It's just hiding in a smarter outfit. Orientation isn't shameful. It's the first act of authorship, and that's the work—not to be in the "right" quadrant but to stop lying to yourself about the one you're in.

The real test begins once the mask is off. The performance doesn't just disappear. It waits. It waits for the moment you're exhausted. It waits for the silence that feels unbearable. It waits for the sign that telling the truth will cost you something. Then it whispers, "Put the mask back on. At least you knew who you were when you wore it."

That is the seduction of reperformance. It's insidious. It's that deep sneaky urge to slide back into the old costume—not because it fits but because it hides. Performance is always waiting, especially when you're exposed. Performance isn't just a behavior. It's a coping mechanism. It's a loop.

Just because you drop the act in one place doesn't mean it won't show up somewhere else. You may tell your team the truth but overexplain it to soften the blow. You say no to a client who's a bad fit and then stay up all night replaying the conversation in your mind, wondering if you should have made the rejection sound nicer. You stop managing perception until someone questions your decision, and suddenly you're back to spinning the story again.

The seduction of reperformance is safety masquerading as

THE COLLAPSE OF THE MASK

strength. Here's the trick: Reperformance feels like control. It feels like stability. It feels like strength, but it's not. It's actually hiding. It's posturing. It's abandonment of self-truth and presence in exchange for approval.

Reflect for a moment on recent interactions. That speech wasn't clarity; it was camouflage. The email wasn't direct; it was a performance in plain clothes. You weren't grounded. You were managing perception again and calling it professionalism. Remember, this isn't judgment. It's merely sobriety.

You will be tempted to make yourself and the way you move in the world palatable again. After raw honesty comes the panic. You told the truth, and no one responded the way you hoped. You took the risk, but the outcome is still uncertain. You stayed with the discomfort, but now your nervous system wants relief. Here is where reperformance sneaks in:

> *Let me just reword that to sound more thoughtful.*
> *Maybe I should soften that statement just in case.*
> *I'll post the version that's even more polished. No need to show the messy middle.*

It's true that the desire to soften isn't weakness. But every time you perform for safety, you teach yourself that truth isn't enough. Over time that "truth" becomes your rhythm. It becomes your identity. That is the moment of choice, not between right or wrong but between comfort and congruence.

Truth without applause is the ultimate defiance. You said the hard thing. You stayed in the fire. You chose the truth, and no one clapped. No one said thank you. No one validated your clarity. No one rescued you from the awkward silence that followed. Now your old reflex kicks in to perform it, spin it, buffer it, or distract from it.

This is the moment when you're most likely to betray yourself, and that's why it matters. No, the applause isn't coming, but neither is the end of the world. You said what needed to be said. Now just stand in it.

That is what real alignment feels like—lonely, clear, and unshakable. You are sitting in the tension of becoming. You are in the pause right before you move forward. You're feeling the aftershocks after you speak plainly, when you hover over *send* and want to reword the email, and as you fight the urge to reperform.

You've dropped the mask. You've stopped performing. You've told the truth, and now you're alone in the quiet. There's no echo chamber, no praise, just your own breath and the silence of integrity. You'll be tempted to backpedal. You'll be seduced to spin it, shrink it, and repackage it. But if you can hold on, if you can let the silence settle without reaching for the mask, you aren't just *saying* you've evolved, you're *proving* it.

PRESENCE AS RESISTANCE

Telling the truth doesn't mean becoming a blunt instrument. This isn't about speaking your mind to feel powerful, prove you're right, or unload your unprocessed anger onto someone else. That's not presence. That's projection. That's ego in raw form. Truth isn't a weapon. It's a responsibility. It requires discernment, timing, and care. If you're using "radical honesty" to dominate a room, you're still performing, just in a louder costume.

Presence means telling the truth in a way that costs you something, not others. It means staying with what's real without using it to punish, persuade, or perform. So don't confuse honesty with aggression. The work isn't to be louder. The work is to be faithful to what you know and to who you're becoming.

THE COLLAPSE OF THE MASK

This is the true meaning of presence. Presence doesn't seek applause. Presence doesn't explain itself. Presence isn't a tactic. It's a stance. Presence isn't calmness. It's defiance. It's choosing to stand in the middle of not knowing, not reaching for the mask, and resisting the urge to perform.

You are in the Forge, not because anything is easy but because you stayed. When you stay long enough, you begin to understand. Maurice Merleau-Ponty wrote, "It is the essence of certainty to be established only with reservations."[46] Certainty isn't the absence of doubt. It's the willingness to act *while still carrying the doubt*. If your clarity feels too clean, it's probably just your old mask—repurposed. The truth doesn't shout. It whispers through the tension you're willing to hold.

Certainty that carries its own reservations, that knows it could be wrong, is strength. Certainty without self-awareness is merely arrogance. It's the difference between "I've committed enough to stand here and be open to move" and "I know; therefore I'm right." The first, not the second, is the kind of certainty we're talking about.

That kind of presence is quiet, but it's heavy. It is not the curated, confident leadership brand of presence so often talked about in organizational development. The presence you want to have sits with uncertainty and doesn't flinch. It's a form of resistance—not resistance as in defiance of others but resistance to the pull to perform, fix, escape, or explain. Presence isn't a tool. It's a way of being.

Presence gets misused all the time. We think it means being calm, neutral, or still. But presence isn't passive. It's the heaviest thing you can hold. Presence is voluntary gravity. It's choosing to stay grounded while the storm tries to lift you out of yourself. It's sitting with what's true without dressing it up or making it palatable.

Presence says things like this: "I won't spend this. I won't reach for relief. I won't perform with a clarity that I don't actually have."

THE RECURRENCE EFFECT

That's not passive; that's power. Sit with this power like a deep breath you hold and don't exhale.

Presence is the most radical form of defiance we can have. When everything in our world pushes us toward polish, speed, and optimization, we choose stillness, truth, and tension. That's a rebellion we want to name. That presence doesn't change the room. It confronts it.

Here's the moment you feel like you're doing nothing but you're actually holding everything. You walk into the meeting and say what's true without wrapping it up. On a strategy call, you show up to the hard conversation and don't overnarrate your intent. You sit with the fallout and don't scramble to be liked.

That's presence, and it takes more strength than any script ever could. Presence without strategy is terrifying, and that's why it matters. Most of us, even the most honest people, still attempt to strategize to our presence. We tell the truth, but we calibrate the tone. We stay silent, but we posture competence. We show up but with a backup plan in our pocket.

The presence we're talking about isn't strategy. It's surrender to what is, not as resignation but as full-contact reality. It means not acting strong so you're not questioned. It's not withholding disappointment to be seen as grateful. It's not using clarity as control instead of contribution. Presence without performance means "I am here, and I don't need to be understood to stay." It's brutal, it's beautiful, and it's rare.

Presence isn't found; it's practiced. No one wakes up one day fully present. It's not a trait we acquire. It's a ritual to practice, especially in the moments when presence feels least possible. Every act of presence is a refusal to abandon yourself, and it shows up in the smallest moves. You don't check your phone when you feel alone. You don't talk over your discomfort with humor. You don't apologize for taking up space with your truth.

That's presence. It's not flashy. It's not public. It's not for show. It's the foundation for anything real. It rejects even subtle forms of performance such as performing humility, performing transparency, and performing peace. Presence is physical—a stillness that resists flight, a breath that holds without explaining, hands that don't fidget in discomfort.

REFLECTION PAUSE

The truth is that you've spent years managing optics. You've learned how to say the "right thing," look the part, and stay in control. But none of that was presence. It was a role, a mask, a performance. Now that role is over. What's left is this: you, unmasked, unarmed, and still there. The work is to sit with what's real, hold your shape without a script, and finally fully arrive with no performance and no applause—just presence. Let's stay here even if it shakes, *especially* if it shakes.

Practice the rhythm of awaken and remember, and return with the following exercises.

◉ AWAKEN

- Where am I still trying to signal authenticity instead of living it?
- What subtle version of performance am I still clinging to for safety?

📍 REMEMBER

- Presence isn't how I feel. It's what I refuse to abandon.
- I don't need to be seen to stay true. I just need to stay.

↩ RETURN

- What would it look like to be fully here without defense, without disguise?
- What rhythm even now will I return to—not to be right but to be real.

IDENTITY AND MOTION—NOT DEFINED BUT LIVED IN

You've collapsed the mask, resisted the urge to reperform, and stood in the raw heat of presence without applause, without payoff. Now we confront one of the most seductive myths in personal growth, that there's a *"real self"* buried somewhere beneath the rubble, just waiting to be discovered, as if identity were a treasure chest, not a trail. There is no self to *find*. There is only the self you *build*, breath by breath, return by return.

Identity isn't revealed in some moment of clarity. It's *declared* in the dark and then *proved* in the daylight of repetition. You don't uncover who you are. You *decide* who you are and then act like it—especially when it would be easier not to.

Comfort. Conditioning. Consensus. There is no authentic self waiting patiently beneath the wreckage. There is only the identity you commit to through recurrence—the one you come back to when the mask has burned, the noise has faded, and no one's watching. That's the hard truth. You don't become someone

THE COLLAPSE OF THE MASK

different by thinking harder. You become someone real by *returning*—again and again—to what matters most, not because it's easy but because it's *yours*.

Identity is proclaimed by what you return to when nobody's watching. You're not leveling up. You're holding your shape even when it's boring, even when no one sees, even when you slip into the Nest and have to crawl back out. You are not your intention; you are your return.

If you have been holding onto some quiet hope that there's a fully formed version of yourself just waiting for you to discover beneath the rubble, hear me say this gently and honestly: There is no authentic hidden self. There's only the self you choose, the self you return to.

You don't discover who you are. You decide. The idea of "finding yourself" is a lie sold to people who are afraid to choose the truth. Identity is a rhythm, not a revelation. You don't stumble into it. You declare it, you test it, and then you return to it again and again, especially when it would be easier not to. You are not a sealed or closed system.

Maurice Merleau-Ponty explained, "Nothing determines me from outside, not because nothing acts upon me, but, on the contrary, because I am from the start outside myself and open to the world."[47] You were never a sealed self trying to survive the world. You were born in relationship. You become through contact. The question isn't how to stay safe. It's how to stay *honest* in the middle of it all.

You don't become by resisting the world. You become by remaining in relationship with it. You need to remember that not everything that shapes you defines you. You are free. You are not here to be untouched. You are here to be in this life, in this world, unfinished, honest, and in motion.

THE RECURRENCE EFFECT

Identity isn't an epiphany. It's a pattern. You are not who you *say* you are. You are what you *do* when it's hard. Your values aren't words you recite. They're what you return to under pressure. Your identity isn't a brand. It's a track record.

Becoming is maintenance, not momentum. Once you stop performing, once you stand in presence, you don't level up. You hold your shape. That's where becoming happens, in the boring decision to return and not betray what you said you cared about, even when no one's watching, even when no one's impressed. What does that look like? It's the decision not to ghost yourself in moments of fatigue. It's the way posture, tone, and truth stack into a new self, not all at once but little by little. It's how identity becomes muscle memory, stance, and rhythm.

You can't perform your way into integrity. You cannot *earn* authenticity. If you're curating identity, performing it, and controlling it, it's not you. It's marketing. You're not a brand; you're a human. If your identity needs to be explained, it hasn't been lived yet. Stop editing yourself for appeal. You don't have to be liked to be real, but you do have to be consistent. Let go of polish and pick up pattern.

Alignment is greater than definition. You're not looking for a clean definition anymore. You're looking for alignment. Ask yourself, "Am I living in a way that reflects what I say matters? Am I returning to the same truths even when they're inconvenient? Am I anchored in values that aren't dependent on my mood?"

Integrity is direction (and devotion), not destination. You don't need a *clear* identity. You need a *lived* one. You don't need to explain yourself. You need to keep showing up in the same way. You're not here to be understood. You're here to be congruent. That is where the recurrence comes in.

The daily return is the evidence of your identity—not the mission statement, not the keynote. The proof is in the walk back to the hard

THE COLLAPSE OF THE MASK

choice, the breath before you tell the truth, the stillness after saying no to what you used to tolerate. Identity is what you come back to, not what you say once. That is how you know what you've committed to becoming and that you're willing to bleed for it.

Here's the brutal truth. You don't *find* who you are. You *forge* it, choice by choice, return by return. Oh, it won't always feel right. It won't always feel real. Some days it won't even feel like *you*. But if you keep showing up the same way, even when it's hard, when no one claps, and especially when you'd rather vanish, that's identity—not a definition but a pattern.

If you're still standing, still showing up raw, still refusing to pick the mask back up, then maybe, just maybe, you haven't become someone else. Maybe you've finally stopped abandoning yourself.

Next we'll look in the mirror, not for approval but to see what's still standing after all this.

THE MIRROR AFTER THE MASK

Let's look again in the mirror. After all, stripping away is not always beautiful, but it is yours. You're standing, not in the Forge or the Cave but in the hallway between who you were and who you are becoming. Here is where you see what you stayed for. We opened this chapter with the quote from Simone de Beauvoir: "I tore myself away from the safe comfort of certainties through my love for truth—and truth rewarded me."[48] This is what it means to stay awake—not to finally feel certain but to live ready to let go of the next thing you're sure of. Truth doesn't settle. It strips. If you're becoming someone worth trusting, that process doesn't end. It returns.

You don't have to like what you see when you look in the

mirror. You just have to not run from it. Look not at what you project, not at what you'd hoped you'd become, but at what's still standing after the fire. This is the mirror after the mask.

This is likely the first time you've seen yourself without strategy. Like amusement park mirrors that bend the truth into funny shapes, we've all looked in mirrors that we knew weren't accurate. Some mirrors we've used are really feedback loops. We learned to shape ourselves based on how others responded. We tweaked the angle. We adjusted the light. We changed what we showed based on what others applauded. But now the performance has ended, the mask has dropped, and the script is gone. Our self-management systems have short-circuited.

Here's what's left: you, unedited, without audience, without reward—that's the only version that matters. You don't see the "real" you. You see the honest you. It's essential that you understand that. Even now you may be struggling with the myth that the "real" you is somehow pure, noble, and integrated. But the truth doesn't always look heroic.

Sometimes it looks exhausted. Sometimes it looks scared. Sometimes it looks like someone who's barely hanging on. But it's still the truth.

You're not polished; you're present. You're not clear; you're committed. You're not fixed—you never needed to be—but you're still here. That's enough.

You might not like what you see, but that doesn't mean it's "wrong." You might look in the mirror and feel shame. You might see remnants of the old mask. You might see contradictions, avoidance, hunger, rage, grief. Good, that's good. That's reality. That's access. This isn't about loving what you see. It's about staying when you don't. This is the deepest test of integrity: Can you witness yourself without retreating?

THE COLLAPSE OF THE MASK

It's okay to feel the emotions of this process. You're allowed to grieve what you've lost, even if it was never really you. You're allowed to feel small as long as you don't disappear. The version of you that's still standing doesn't need to be impressive. It just needs to be honest.

The mirror isn't a judgment. It's a recommitment. You aren't evaluating yet. That comes next. This is about reverence. This is witnessing. It's not about measuring how far you've come. It's about noticing what you refuse to abandon.

What you see in the mirror now is who you stayed for. This is who you're still becoming. This is the version of you that you didn't abandon when it got hard. Presence meets pattern and meets reflection, and what emerges is authorship. There's no story and no spin, just this: "I'm still here, and I'm not going back."

Sit with yourself. Don't rush your emotions. Feel the ache of exposure and the sacredness of not retreating. This is a moment of pause, a moment after the collapse, after the fire, after the temptation to go back when you look in the mirror and finally see yourself. It's not who you thought you'd be, not who you pretended to be, and not what others expected—just yourself, flawed, shaken, awake, and still choosing to return.

There's no applause, no clarity, and no payoff—just presence, just breath, just you and the decision to not abandon yourself. This is the mirror after the mask. You're in the threshold between Experiment and Evaluate. It's time to ask the question you've earned the right to ask: "What did all of this do to me?" This is the moment you stop trying to make sense of it all and finally start listening to what it made of you.

Once you've seen it, you can't unsee it. You've moved. You've collapsed the performance. You've resisted return. You've stood in presence and lived your way back into something that might become identity. This isn't resolution. This is recognition.

THE RECURRENCE EFFECT

Colombian writer Gabriel García Márquez wrote, "Human beings are not born once and for all on the day their mothers give birth to them, but . . . life obliges them over and over again to give birth to themselves."[49] This wasn't a breakdown. It was a rebirth, and another one is coming, not because you failed but because you're *still becoming*. The work isn't to protect who you *were*. It's to stay present enough to bring the next version of yourself into the world—no matter the cost.

You've been born again through fire, not fate. Now it's time to look back, not to assess but to witness, not to ask "Did it work?" but to ask "What did it do to me?" You've moved, not just physically, not just behaviorally, but something in you—deep, old, and sacred—finally shifted. You collapsed the mask. You faced the silence. You resisted the urge to turn it into a story too soon. You held presence. You chose alignment over approval. You didn't run. That matters, not because it was impressive but because it was honest.

RETURN FROM THE DRIFT

Something is different now—not better, not solved, just different. You've stopped chasing clarity. You've stopped trying to be understood. You've started to recognize yourself again, not as a role but as a rhythm. You can't unsee that now.

◉ AWAKEN

- Where am I still waiting to be rescued by clarity or applause?
- Where have I been expecting arrival instead of witnessing change?

THE COLLAPSE OF THE MASK

📍 REMEMBER

- My identity isn't something I find. It's what I return to under pressure.
- The version of me I see now is unfinished and still worthy of allegiance.

↩ RETURN

- What rhythm will I keep returning to even when it's not impressive?
- What does staying true look like now that I've dropped the mask?

The next phase of your evolution is subtle and sacred, not because you've earned the right to evaluate but because you've suffered enough to know that reflection isn't feedback. It's fidelity. The next chapter is where you measure how far you've come. It's where you honor the cost of becoming someone who can move like this at all.

You want to witness what the fire took and what it reveals. What are you still carrying that isn't yours anymore? That's where we go next—not to analyze, not to optimize, but to reencounter yourself in the smoke, in the stillness, and in the aftermath of a truth.

Truth lived all the way through.

PART III

EVALUATE

(WITH CANDOR)

CHAPTER 7

REFLECTION IS WHERE MEANING BEGINS

*Thinking does not lead to truth; truth
is the beginning of thought.*

HANNAH ARENDT

You have emerged from the fire like a phoenix rising from the ashes. It's time to look at yourself and see who you really are. It's time for Evaluation.

We've been conditioned to treat Evaluation as a postmortem of what went wrong after something dies. But nothing has gone wrong, and you are most certainly alive. Instead, we need to use Evaluation as a breakdown of what worked, what didn't, and how we optimize for the next time.

THE RECURRENCE EFFECT

Hannah Arendt's quote above about truth being where thought begins flips that preconditioned approach to thought on its head. Truth isn't something we arrive at by thinking. It's what jolts us into thought. After that jolt is the aftermath, the quiet moment when the noise clears and something lingers. What you do with that truth—how long you stay with it, how deeply you witness it—is what matters now.

Most people move too quickly after the fire. They want to make what they've been through useful. They want the moral of the story. They want to extract the value and leave the mess behind. But real evaluation doesn't just ask, "What did I learn?" It asks, "What did this cost me? What did it burn away? What remains after the performance is gone?"

Evaluation is an invitation to a sacred act of devotion. It's about reverence, a reverence that begins when truth interrupts your life and refuses to leave. You are here to witness a reckoning. This kind of evaluation isn't intellectual. It lives in your breath, your behavior, and your return.

Being a witness is the act of seeing without solving, of being present without performing, of allowing what you've endured or what you've done to fully exist in your awareness without rushing to justify it or change it. It's not about interpreting, explaining, or fixing. To witness is to stay in relationship with what is real without softening it, spinning it, or turning it away.

Meaning doesn't emerge from analysis. It emerges from attention and from allegiance to what hurts, what changed, and what still refuses to let go of you. That's what we mean by Evaluate. Stop chasing clarity, and stop trying to package the experience. Just stand still long enough to see what the fire made of you before trying to turn it into a lesson.

That's what devotion looks like. It's not about what you know

REFLECTION IS WHERE MEANING BEGINS

now; it's about what you refuse to unsee and how you carry it forward from this point. Here's the rub. There's part of you that wants to "know," to wrap this into insight, to declare something definitive. That desire for certainty isn't weakness; it's just ancient. It's your nervous system doing its job, but what got you here won't get you where you want to be.

Witnessing is what makes the process honest. It's the refusal to soften, to spin, to move too quickly toward clarity. You don't use the mirror to validate where you are or who you are. You face it to confront what you're still becoming. Witnessing is the discipline of staying in relationship with what the mirror shows, even when it shakes your sense of self. Witnessing is the sacred opposition of avoidance. It's not passive. It's a discipline, and it's where all honest Evaluation begins.

Evaluation isn't a wrap-up. It certainly isn't a list of lessons learned. We're not here to debrief. We're here to witness. This chapter begins in the aftermath, not the part with takeaways and clarity. Right now, the smoke from the fire is still in your lungs. The quiet feels heavier than the chaos that came before. You don't know what's next, but you do know something powerful, and that is that you won't go back—and that's enough.

Evaluation is a vigil. You don't break it down like a debrief or a dissection. You stand with it. You honor what got burned away and what didn't. There's no applause and no insight to impress anyone. There's just you staying long enough to see what's still standing, and that's sacred ground.

You don't owe a takeaway to what you've been through. You don't owe this experience a bullet point. You don't need a headline to justify what it cost you. This is the shift. You owe it your attention, your stillness, and your willingness to stay because what you just walked through, whatever it was, has already shaped you. If you move too quickly, you'll miss what the experience was trying to give you.

Here's the tension: Your brain will beg for closure. It wants to collapse this into something neat, resolved, and *known*. That's convergent thinking—the instinct to narrow, to finalize, to reduce ambiguity. But real reflection asks something harder. It invites divergent thinking—the willingness to open, to expand, to hold multiple truths without forcing them into a single answer. That's what makes this sacred. It's not arriving at clarity but resisting the demand for it. When you resist the rush to converge on a single answer, you're not lost. You're learning to stay with what your nervous system once called unsafe.

This isn't about meaning. It's about letting meaning emerge slowly and honestly, without force. We aren't writing a report. We're meditating on a prayer. Let silence be part of your reflection.

After the fire, you are sitting alone in a quiet room, still trembling. You've survived something, and it changed you. This is not the moment to build a plan. This is the moment to tell the truth about what's still smoldering inside you. No fix. No spin. Just reverence. That's where we begin to reflect, not with answers but with attention.

THE LEARNING KNOWING MIRROR

Evaluation begins when you stop clinging to *knowing* and start humbling yourself to *learning*. That's why the mirror for Evaluation is the Learning Knowing Mirror. In this chapter, you will reflect on it as a test of presence. Anytime you try to convert uncertainty into control, it reminds you that knowing is about protecting

REFLECTION IS WHERE MEANING BEGINS

identity and learning is about allowing, even encouraging, that identity to evolve.

KNOWING (certainty as identity)	LEARNING (humble participation)
"I know. I am this."	"I am always becoming."
Safety · Control · Closure Amygdala calms	Uncertainty · Growth · Effort Neuroplasticity activates

The Learning Knowing Mirror sharpens this moment of witnessing. It doesn't just reflect what you've experienced. It reveals the choice you're making in real time. Will you cling to the safety of knowing or stay open to the discomfort of learning? We want tidy narratives and clean frameworks. But real reflection is not about explanation; it's about integration. It's not "What did I learn?" Instead, it asks, "What did this do to me? What no longer fits? What do I see now that I can't unsee?"

Integration means letting it rearrange you, not package you. This is where the Learning Knowing Mirror shows up, sometimes gently, sometimes with a gut punch. You feel it when you start asking, "What does this mean?" before you've even finished feeling it. That rush to meaning is not curiosity. It's an attempt to escape.

Our brains are wired to seek certainty because uncertainty feels like a threat.[50] Our brains are wired for survival, not truth. Certainty feels like safety, and the moment we feel uncertain, our threat-detection systems light up. Our brain doesn't know if we're being chased by a lion or challenged by feedback. It just tells us that *something is wrong*.

THE RECURRENCE EFFECT

When we default to knowing, we do so because knowing feels like control, and control feels like survival. This isn't a weakness. It's our wiring. The problem is that evolution only got us here. *Intention* is what will carry us forward and allow us to evolve.

The Learning Knowing Mirror (shown below) is a continuum that moves from Knowing (Certainty as Identity) to Learning (Humble Participation). When you're in the Knowing stage, you may feel calm and unthreatened. The certainty you believe you have tells your brain there are no threats present.

Moving away from Knowing, the next stage is Reinforced Assumption. Here you are beginning to feel some dissonance between what you see reflected in the mirror and what you believe to be true about yourself. Your brain will attempt to reduce the dissonance through confirmation bias, accepting input that supports what you believe and rejecting what challenges it.

The middle stage of the Learning Knowing Mirror is Cognitive Dissonance. At this point, the lack of alignment between your reflection and your beliefs about yourself makes you feel anxious. Your brain tries to create new meaning from the feedback.

Moving closer to Learning is the stage of Emerging Awareness. Here you begin to admit you might have been wrong before. Your brain works on overriding your default biases. This step takes work on your part, and you may feel fatigued from the effort.

The final stage on the continuum is Learning. Here you are more comfortable with, or better able to tolerate, uncertainty. Your brain is able to make new connections and pathways, equipping you for growth.

REFLECTION IS WHERE MEANING BEGINS

STAGE	DESCRIPTION	BRAIN/BEHAVIOR NOTE
KNOWING (CERTAINTY AS IDENTITY)	"I know this. I am this."	Amygdala calms when certainty is present. Identity is protected.
REINFORCED ASSUMPTION	"It's worked before, it must still be true."	Confirmation bias filters reality to reduce dissonance.
COGNITIVE DISSONANCE	"Something doesn't add up."	Dissonance triggers anxiety; prefrontal cortex starts negotiating new meaning.
LEARNING (HUMBLE PARTICIPATION)	"I am always becoming."	Neuroplasticity in action. Growth mindset and uncertainty tolerance expand.

Your nervous system isn't built for nuance. It's built for escape routes. In this moment after the fire, the threat is gone. You're not being chased. You're being changed. You're not here to survive your life. You're here to learn from it. Evaluation invites you to sit in the fire—to feel the threat without flinching, to breathe through the bias, and to wait until the smoke clears. Only then do you see what knowing tried to hide. If you can sit in this moment of reflection without reaching for answers, you're learning.

CANDOR IS THE COMPASS

You've sat with the aftermath and honored the fire. Now comes the moment that many people would rather skip: candor. But you can't bypass candor because reflection without honesty isn't reflection. It's performance. It's just another mask. Eventually, you have to stop admiring the smoke and start naming the burn.

You can't evaluate what you won't name. You can't shift what you refuse to see. You can't reorient around something when you're still spinning. Candor is what breaks the spell. Candor is not brutal honesty for shock value. It's not confession as performance. Instead, it's clear-eyed naming without drama, without deflection.

Candor is asking, "What didn't work? What cost too much? What was I pretending not to know?" This isn't about judgment. It's about access. If you can't name it, you can't move through it—period. Candor keeps reflection from becoming strategic knowing, building a narrative that keeps us in control.

Candor lives on the other side of the Learning Knowing Mirror. It's the part where you say, "Maybe I was wrong. Maybe I'm still wrong. Maybe I won't know for a while." That's not weakness; that's learning. It only happens when you stop trying to protect your current identity with polished insights.

German-American philosopher Paul Tillich wrote, "The courage to be is the courage to accept oneself, in spite of being unacceptable."[51] That's what it takes, not just admitting you got it wrong but facing the parts of yourself you've worked hardest to hide. The impulse to spin, to soften, to suppress—all of that lives in the fear that what's inside you is unworthy. Candor is what interrupts that fear. It says, "Even this version of me deserves to be seen, *especially* this one." So the *courage to be* is not the courage to fix, prove, or transcend yourself. It's the courage to *stand fully in your existence*—even when it hurts, even when everything in you says you shouldn't be here, even when you don't like what you see in the mirror. It's the refusal to abandon yourself, not *after* you've become acceptable but right now—*because you are.*

REFLECTION IS WHERE MEANING BEGINS

Candor often gets misused. Honesty is a skill, not a spill. It's not about dumping everything raw and calling it "truth." It's a discipline, a muscle. It's the practice of saying what's true in a way that's useful, clean, and unbuffered. Candor is not about being right. It's not about being liked. It's about being aligned. Candor doesn't shout. It clarifies, and clarity is compassion even when it cuts.

Without candor, reflection becomes censorship. Going a little deeper, the real danger here isn't lying to others. It's lying to yourself in subtle, polished ways that *feel* productive. When you frame your failure as a lesson, you tell yourself that the discomfort was worth it before you even sat in it. You explain away the misalignment as part of the process, but that's not reflection. That's identity and reputation management, and it keeps you stuck.

Candor is what breaks that cycle. It says, "Here's where I betrayed what I said mattered. Here's where I abandoned what I claim to believe." Candor doesn't flinch. It allows you to stand in front of the mirror and say what you've avoided saying. Where reverence is stillness, candor is orientation. This is the first time you speak plainly, not to impress, not to convince, but because you're finally willing to know what's true. From this raw, clear ground, meaning actually begins.

THE FRICTION OF REORIENTATION

You told the truth. You named what hurt. You saw what you couldn't unsee, and now, quite honestly, you feel worse. That's not failure; that's friction. This is the part no one tells you about. Clarity doesn't feel clean. It doesn't bring closure. It doesn't come with a map. It just removes the option to pretend, and now you're stuck between two worlds: the old one that no longer fits and the new one you haven't built yet. Welcome into your own liminal container—a deliberate space held open between what was and what's becoming, where old identities loosen, clarity isn't rushed, and transformation is allowed to unfold without performance.

You're not who you were, but you're not sure who you are. This is the identity limbo. After you've dropped the mask, after you've named what wasn't true, you're left in a raw, undefined space. The reflex is to rebuild fast—pick a new path, a new persona, or a new plan. But you're not supposed to feel certain right now. You're supposed to feel unmoored because you've outgrown something, and growth never feels like certainty. It feels like dissonance, like sitting between coordinates that no longer align. This isn't regression. It's an orientation that's recalibrating itself in real time.

Spanish philosopher Miguel de Unamuno is credited with saying, "The skeptic does not mean him who doubts, but him who investigates or researches, as opposed to him who asserts and thinks that he has found." You're not in doubt. You're in investigation. You're in Evaluation. The ache isn't confusion; it's contact. You're not collapsing. You're confronting. That is what happens when you stop asserting and start saying what's real without knowing where it leads. What de Unamuno was pointing to is the cost of not defaulting to a false clarity.

Reorientation isn't clarity. It's a willingness to turn. Reorientation isn't about seeing the whole road. It's about noticing that you're facing the wrong direction and turning, not with a plan, not with confidence, but with integrity. You're not choosing a destination. You're choosing to stop betraying what you now know, even if it's foggy, even if it's slow, even if it's lonely. That's what turning feels like. It's not triumphant but exposed and fragile, like choosing alignment before it pays off.

REFLECTION IS WHERE MEANING BEGINS

The dissonance you feel means you've moved. That strange, off-kilter, or shaky feeling is not confusion. It's not regression. It's proof—proof that you're no longer moving from default, proof that you've stopped chasing applause and started chasing congruence.

Reorientation always comes with discomfort because you're walking away from a rhythm you used to call home, even if it hurts. That ache in your chest, that floating sensation—that's what realignment feels like before it becomes rhythm. So you have to stay with it. What you're feeling is cognitive dissonance. That's your body letting go of knowing and stepping into learning. Your brain is wired to resolve dissonance fast—to close the gap, to restore coherence—even if it means retreating into old beliefs. But if you can resist that reflex, you create the space where your evolution can begin.

The Learning Knowing Mirror lights up in this space because that is where your stories get disrupted. The certainty that once gave you a sense of self now feels suffocating. If you stay here in the tension without collapsing into a new false clarity, your new self begins to emerge.

REFLECTION PAUSE

You don't need to know where you're going. You just need to stop heading where you can't stay. That's what this moment is—not a new path but a new posture, a willingness to say, "I don't know what's next, but I know what I'm done with." That's how reorientation begins now with confidence, candor, and a quiet turn.

👁 AWAKEN

- Where am I still trying to explain instead of witness?
- What have I been avoiding naming because it might mean I have to change?

📍 REMEMBER

- Reflection isn't reaction. It's responsibility.
- Once I've seen it, I can't pretend I haven't, and that truth demands something of me.

↩ RETURN

- What will I refuse to look away from, even if it's inconvenient?
- How will I reorient what's true, not what's comfortable?

MEANING ISN'T MINED—IT'S MADE

Most of us expect meaning to arrive like a message in a bottle, but it doesn't come with answers. Spanish philosopher José Ortega y Gasset wrote, "To be surprised, to wonder, is to begin to understand."[52] This is where most people get stuck. They wait for meaning to arrive like it's buried treasure. If they dig deep enough into their pain, they think clarity will pop out and explain everything. But that's a lie. Meaning doesn't show up. It doesn't reveal itself. It's not something you find. It's something you make—not from control, not from certainty, but from your willingness to respond with intention to what happened.

You don't find meaning. You make it. Wonder is how you know

REFLECTION IS WHERE MEANING BEGINS

you're on the right track. Meaning comes with wonder. It comes in the surprise of how you've moved through something hard with quiet integrity, saying no when yes would have been easier. It's the unseen choice to stay aligned even when no one was watching.

There is no "Aha!" moment coming to justify your discomfort and no perfect insight that ties it all together. If you're waiting for that, you're still outsourcing meaning to something outside yourself. That's not authorship; that's avoidance. You're not here to uncover a moral to the story. You're here to decide what story you now live into. That's the only way forward.

You make meaning by how you move after the fire. Meaning is forged through what comes next. It's the stance you take, not the story you tell. You make meaning by what you do when the applause stops, the ache still lingers, and you act in alignment anyway. It doesn't feel profound. It just feels honest.

Meaning doesn't show up on the Knowing side of the mirror. It doesn't come from "getting it right." It comes from showing up to what's real again and again without needing it to resolve. The Learning Knowing Mirror reveals your impulse to make pain productive, to turn becoming into branding. But learning demands that you stay in the ambiguity long enough to let it rewrite you, not just inform you.

Meaning is not a message. It's a movement. The goal here isn't distilling your pain into a sound bite. You're orienting your life around what's now undeniable. Meaning is not what you say this experience meant. It's what you refuse to unsee and how you move because of it. That is authorship, not articulation. You don't need to name it perfectly. You just need to let it change you visibly. That's meaning—not a message, but a movement.

What happened isn't the meaning. How you carry it, that's the meaning. You've got the raw material now, not the story, the scar, the shift, or the signal. What you do with it is yours to decide. You don't find meaning. You make it brick by brick, action by action, day by unremarkable day. That's the work.

THE DISCIPLINE OF STAYING HONEST

The fire has gone out, and you are alone—just you, the ashes, and what you choose to build from here. This is where the work starts to get quiet again. You've had the collapse. You've named what's real. You've started to move with intention. Now comes the repetition, the return. This is the discipline of staying honest.

Reflection without return is rumination. If you don't do something with what you've seen, you're just loitering in your own awareness. The point isn't to become more self-aware. The point is to become more self-aligned. The question isn't "What did I learn?" but "Will I live differently because of it? Will I stay honest now that no one's asking me to be?" That's the test.

Rollo May wrote, "Freedom is the possibility of development, of enhancement of one's life or the possibility of withdrawing, shutting oneself up, denying and stultifying one's growth."[53] That's what's really on the line here—not just your *truth* but your *freedom*. Freedom isn't the absence of constraint. It's your capacity to choose what kind of life you continue to live. Stay honest or shut yourself off. Return or retreat. The discipline is the difference.

Staying honest is a daily act, not a peak experience. We've been trained to treat breakthroughs like finish lines, but staying honest isn't a climax. It's maintenance. It's how you respond when you're exhausted, when you're misunderstood, or when you're tempted to perform just one more time. This isn't a motivational speech. This is your new floor. Staying honest isn't about courage

REFLECTION IS WHERE MEANING BEGINS

anymore. It's about consistency, and that's what changes you. This isn't the fire but rather the rhythm you commit to after the fire.

Integrity is what you keep doing after it stops being inspiring. This is the brutal edge. Most people can tell the truth *once*. Most people can resist the mask *for a moment*. But staying honest, staying congruent *every day* when it's boring, when it's costly, and when it's not poetic or postable—that's the difference between transformation and theater. That is where integrity is no longer an idea. It's a track record, and it's built one quiet, invisible decision at a time.

The fire changed you. The reflection revealed something, and the meaning started to take shape. But none of that matters if you don't return, if you don't keep telling the truth after the stakes are low, after the spotlight fades, after the story feels old. Staying honest isn't an event. It's a discipline that turns meaning into movement. Not once. Every. Single. Time.

This is your rhythm now. It's not dramatic or loud; it's real. The Knowing reflex wants to believe you've changed, but only Learning returns. Only Learning says, "I'm not done. I'm still listening." The Learning Knowing Mirror doesn't show you how far you've come. It asks if you'll keep coming back when there's nothing new to see, only the discipline of staying honest.

THE MIRROR IS NOT THE ANSWER; IT'S AN ONGOING ENCOUNTER

Carl Jung said, "Your vision will become clear only when you can look into your heart. Who looks outside, dreams; who looks inside, awakens." You've walked through the aftermath. You've told the truth. You've turned. You've moved. You've stayed honest. Now before this chapter ends, we return to the mirror, not for answers but for a reckoning that doesn't resolve, because this isn't

THE RECURRENCE EFFECT

the mirror that says, "You're done." This is the one that whispers, "Are you still there?"

The mirror doesn't close the chapter. It reopens it. Most people think reflection ends with a takeaway, a lesson, a line, or a summary they can share, but real reflection doesn't offer closure. It offers confrontation again and again. You'll move forward, but the image stays with you—the one you saw when the mask came off, the one that wasn't curated or cleaned. That mirror now lives in you. You see it when you're tempted to perform. You hear it when you start to soften the truth. You feel it in your gut when you're about to trade congruence for comfort. The mirror didn't end anything. It started something.

Reflection that doesn't change you is strategy, not truth. It's *your* reflection. If your reflection becomes a story you tell instead of a standard you live, you're not evolving. You're strategizing. You're still curating clarity instead of walking in it. You're still seeking applause for your insight instead of letting it humble you. The mirror can't save you from your patterns. It can only show you what they cost. What do you do next? That's where truth earns its name.

The mirror is a relationship, not a moment. You don't just check in once. You keep returning, even when it's quiet, even when the image hasn't changed, even when you wish it would say something new. Reflection isn't a flash of insight. It's a slow, brutal loyalty to what you saw the first time you stopped pretending. That relationship deepens with each return because the mirror doesn't demand performance. It demands presence. It asks, "Will you stay with what you see even when it never applauds you?"

That's the work, to stop asking the mirror to rescue you and start asking it to refine you. This is the deepest turn. You stop using the mirror to validate what you already know and start letting it show you what you're still refusing to learn. That's the

REFLECTION IS WHERE MEANING BEGINS

true shift when the mirror becomes not a confirmation of identity but an invitation to dismantle it and rebuild it.

RETURN FROM THE DRIFT

You don't graduate from reflection. You grow inside it. Every time you revisit what you see, every time you ask yourself if you're still living it, every time you resist the urge to explain yourself away, you become more aligned, more honest, and more real. The mirror is still with you. If you're brave enough to keep looking, it will keep telling the truth.

👁 AWAKEN

- Where am I still mistaking reflection for resolution?
- Have I stopped looking in the mirror because I won't like what it shows me?

📍 REMEMBER

- Meaning isn't something to find. It's what I choose to live into every day.
- The mirror will never lie to me, but I can lie to myself by looking away.

↩ RETURN

- How will I keep coming back to the truth I've already seen without explanation, without performance?

THE RECURRENCE EFFECT

○ What action proves that I haven't abandoned what I claimed mattered most?

You saw what the mirror shows, and you stayed. You made it through the fire. You named what the mask was hiding. You turned even when there was no map. You authored meaning, not because it was obvious but because it was yours to make. You chose to stay honest even when it stopped being impressive. Here you are, not at the end of reflection but at the beginning of a relationship with it. Now you know the mirror doesn't speak once; it whispers every day, "Are you still there?"

From here on, your integrity will be measured by how often you return—not when it's easy, not when it's urgent, but when it's quiet. What you see now you're accountable to, and you don't get to unknow it. So you won't ask, "What did I learn?" Instead, you'll ask, "What am I refusing to look away from?"

This wasn't just a moment; it was a shift. This is where this chapter leaves you, not with clarity but with commitment; not with applause, but with alignment; not with answers, but with the discipline of staying true, even when it's quiet. You don't close the book on reflection. You carry it with you, and now it walks beside you.

You've stayed. You've seen. You've named. You've returned. Now comes the part you can't control: the Evolution. It won't look like progress. It won't feel like momentum. It won't follow a straight line because growth doesn't obey your schedule. It breaks your rhythm. It humbles your timeline and asks, "Can you stay faithful to what matters, even when nothing makes sense?" The next chapter is where we find out.

CHAPTER 8

NO ONE GROWS IN STRAIGHT LINES

One can choose to go back toward safety or forward toward growth. Growth must be chosen again and again; fear must be overcome again and again.

ABRAHAM MASLOW

Let's start with the lie—the one we've all swallowed that told us growth looks like a steady climb, like we're climbing a mountain, constantly moving upward. We expect our growth trajectory to be step-by-step up and to the right—more insight, more achievement, more ease. Everybody's heard the success story with bullet points, the self-improvement arc with perfect pacing, and the graph that never dips and just ascends. But if that were true, you'd be there by now.

As we've discussed, growth is a J-curve. We can't hop from mountaintop to mountaintop without going down into the valley. It doesn't work like that. We want growth to be a straight shot, a clean arc that curves upward with each step, but that's a fantasy. Real growth is jagged. It doubles back. Sometimes it's two steps forward, three steps back. Growth stalls. It demands detours and dead-ends.

Every time it gets hard, we're faced with that same decision to turn back toward comfort or lean forward into discomfort. There is no once and for all breakthrough. There's only choosing again and again and again. But here you are. You're still circling, still struggling, still coming back to the same questions you thought you answered already. That doesn't mean you're failing; it means you're human.

This chapter isn't about how to grow. It's about how to keep choosing growth when it would be easier not to. Part of what we have to overcome is our wiring because our brains are programmed evolutionarily for one thing: to keep us safe. As a result, our brains perceive the process of growing as a true risk to our well-being. Our brain's protective instinct gets triggered when we do something that would have gotten us thrown out of the clan or the group, which would have meant death.

We're really fighting our instincts. We're fighting to be the conductor on the train and not a passenger. We have to confront the cultural fantasy of linear growth. In this chapter, we'll use the Learning Knowing Mirror as a behavioral reality check, not as a belief system validator.

Despite how it seems, conviction does not equal growth. We love conviction. It feels like progress, like clarity, like arrival, but conviction without conduct is just branding. Scottish philosopher Thomas Carlyle said, "Conviction is worthless unless it is converted into conduct." We love the idea of linear progress, but that story collapses the moment we're forced to live with what we say we know.

Conviction feels like growth, but without action, it's just a narrative. The Learning Knowing Mirror doesn't care what you *believe*. It shows you how to *behave*. That's where the truth starts. You can believe all the right things, say all the right things, and even teach them, but until your actions reflect your beliefs, you haven't grown. You've just memorized a better story.

The mirror reveals what narrative hides. That is where the Learning Knowing Mirror enters, not as a metaphor but as a measurement. It doesn't care what you believe; it shows you how you behave. It doesn't ask, "Did you grow?" It asks, "How do you know?"—not in your head, not on paper, but in practice, in motion, and in moments that cost you something. That's where the truth starts—not in clarity but in contradiction, and the gap between what you say matters to you and what you actually protect through your actions.

Reflection isn't a reward. It's a reckoning. Here's the uncomfortable part. Most people use reflection as a reward. *Look how far I've come. Look what I know now. Look how aligned I seem.* But reflection, real reflection, doesn't flatter you; it confronts you. It shows you the shape of your becoming, not as a critique but as an invitation.

The mirror doesn't lie, but it doesn't accuse either. It invites you to see the shape of your becoming. That's the shift from narrative to pattern, from insight to evidence, from passive to active. Growth isn't what you post. It's what you repeat when no one's watching. If what you repeat doesn't match what you profess, you're not evolving. You're rehearsing.

THE RECURRENCE EFFECT

Becoming is about your shape, not your story. So let's just drop the storyline here. You're not a case study. You're a pattern. You're not ascending a staircase. You're circling through your own becoming. The Learning Knowing Mirror doesn't measure your beliefs. It reflects your posture, your presence, your pattern, what you've been doing, what you've been avoiding, and what you keep coming back to. That's where growth shows up—not in the straight line but in the spiral. That's where we begin.

GROWTH HAS A RHYTHM, NOT A ROUTE

The shipwreck isn't the end. It's the signal. In the wreckage is where your map stops working, where your carefully held truth starts to shake, where your carefully crafted story collapses under the weight of reality. Here's the truth: The collapse, the fracture, and the shipwreck are not mistakes. They're a moment of revelation. German-Swiss psychiatrist and philosopher Karl Jaspers said, "Every truth that we may think complete will prove itself untruth at the moment of shipwreck."[54] You didn't evolve through clarity, You evolved through chaos. That's where the rhythm begins.

After the shipwreck, you don't need a map. You need a metronome. We've been taught to look for a plan—something to follow, something to climb. But what if the shape of your growth isn't a path? What if it's a pulse? Here's what we've learned by now. Explore cracks. The surface Experiment shatters the illusion. Only Evaluate reveals the rhythm that's always been playing underneath—not forward, not upward, but through again and again. You don't need clear steps. You need better listening to the beat of your own becoming.

NO ONE GROWS IN STRAIGHT LINES

The mirror doesn't measure you. It keeps time with you. That is where the Learning Knowing Mirror shifts. It's not a report card. It's a metronome. It doesn't ask for your best moments. It reflects your consistent ones—the ones you didn't post, the ones that keep showing up in your posture, your tone, and your choices—because that's the pattern of your life, not the intention but the repetition. Every pass through the mirror shows you what's real, what's habit, what's performative, and what's yours. That's the rhythm we're after—not the noise of ambition but the steady drumbeat of alignment.

Let's return to the shipwreck. When your plan crumbles, when your performance stops working, when the story you've been telling yourself doesn't hold together anymore, that's not the end. That's the invitation. What's left after the shipwreck is what's real and what's true. That's the beginning of rhythm—the slow, often uncomfortable honesty of what you keep returning to, not what you've said mattered or what your life actually honors. When you listen closely, you realize you've been keeping time all along. Now you're just willing to hear it.

Stop looking for the trail. Start noticing the tempo. Growth doesn't come from finding a better map. It comes from recognizing the beat beneath the shipwreck, the pattern beneath the pivot, and the rhythm beneath the wreckage. The map isn't the territory, and someone else's path can't carry your truth.[55] Their coordinates won't decode your rhythm, and their trail was never made for your feet.

You don't evolve in straight lines. You evolve in spirals, in returns, in refrains, and in the recurrence. The mirror doesn't give you direction. It gives you timing. If you can sync with that rhythm, you stop chasing progress and start moving in alignment.

THE RECURRENCE EFFECT

SIGNS YOU'RE STILL BECOMING

What you're feeling is not failure. It's feedback. You're circling back. You're frustrated. You thought you'd be done with this pattern by now, but here it is again, and your brain starts whispering, "I must be failing." But what if you're not? What if this isn't backsliding but becoming? What if what you're feeling is the resistance of someone moving? Returning is not repeating. It can't be because you're not the same person you were the last time you were here. You bring new context, new awareness, and new questions—and that changes everything. What you're in isn't regression; it's recursion. If you can stay with it, that's where the real shift begins.

The wrong mistakes keep you stuck. The right ones stretch you. American jazz pianist Thelonious Monk said, "You've been making the wrong mistakes." Most people hear that and ask, "Are there *right* mistakes?" Yes, there are because growth doesn't mean eliminating error. It means refining it. It means shifting from reactive flailing to intentional friction. Wrong mistakes keep you stuck in the loop. Right mistakes move the loop forward. You're still messing up, but now it's in the direction of learning. Now it's pointing somewhere. That's not failure. That's feedback.

Friction is a signpost, not a stop sign. Here's what most of us call failure, uncertainty, emotional whiplash, repetition, exhaustion, or doubt. But none of those are red lights. They're just signals. If you're paying attention, they tell you exactly where your life is misaligned—where what you say doesn't match what you do, where what you know and how you show up are still intentions. That's not something to escape. That's where the work is.

The mirror makes the mess meaningful. That is where the Learning Knowing Mirror becomes diagnostic, not to shame you and or polish you but to help you notice when you're making the same moves with different stories. It's where the discomfort actually points to growth and where the mess isn't chaos but creation. The mirror reflects what's changed but also what still hasn't. That's where the work is. The mirror doesn't demand perfection. It demands presence, not to clean things up but to stay long enough to see the difference between spiraling out and spiraling forward.

REFLECTION PAUSE

You're not stuck if you're aware of it. If you're circling back again, don't flinch. Don't run. Just ask better questions. "Am I making the same mistake or a more honest one? Is this discomfort directionless, or is it stretching something in me that used to collapse?" That's the real test. If you're still struggling but with more honesty, awareness, and intention, then you're not stuck. You're becoming.

👁 AWAKEN

- Where am I mistaking discomfort for failure instead of feedback?
- What part of my pattern feels chaotic but might actually be a signal that life shifted?

📍 REMEMBER

- Friction doesn't mean I'm broken; it means I'm still becoming.
- The mirror doesn't judge the message. It shows whether it's starting to mean something.

↩ RETURN

- What recurring frustration could be pointing to a deeper alignment I haven't honored yet?
- Where am I flinching from the right mistake because it costs me something real?

RETURN ISN'T STARTING OVER; IT'S STARTING FROM WHERE YOU ARE

If you're honest, you'll see you are not the same. So let's clear this up once and for all. You're not starting over, even if it feels like you are. Even if it looks that way from the outside, you're not regressing. You're recurring, but you're not the same. That's not a cop-out. That's the truth if you're willing to tell it. Russian novelist Fyodor Dostoevsky wrote, "Above all, don't lie to yourself."[56] Return only feels like failure when you're pretending you're not different.

Lying about where you are creates looping. What really traps us is confusing presence with failure. We think, "I'm back here again, which must mean I haven't moved," but that's not true unless you're lying to yourself about how much you've evolved; lying about what you're still carrying; or lying about what you're avoiding, downplaying, or dressing up as progress. When you lie to yourself long enough, you lose the ability to tell what's real—not just out there but inside yourself. That's what Dostoevsky meant.

Self-deception is the beginning of disorientation. You can't orient yourself unless you're honest with yourself about where you are. Too often in our society we want transformational progress. We want instantaneous results. We want hacks. We think things should be done more quickly. We tell ourselves, "If

I keep returning to something, I'm failing because I'm not moving forward fast enough." That's an insidious lie.

The Learning Knowing Mirror isn't a scoreboard. It's a signal. What it shows us is not judgment but evidence. You've been here before, yes, but now you see differently. You speak differently. You choose differently. You've been here before, but you're not who you were. That's not a loop. That's evolution.

The mirror doesn't measure how fast you're moving. It reflects how aligned you are as you move. Don't focus on speed. Focus instead on alignment because alignment will reveal your posture, your presence, and your pattern. If you can face it without flinching, you realize you're not restarting. You're reentering the awareness.

Return is the shape of real growth. As we've seen, real growth isn't a sprint; it's a spiral. You keep coming back to the same terrain from a deeper altitude, a different angle, and a wider understanding. Return is sacred. It's not a sign of failure. It's a signal that you're still in it, still listening, still willing, and still becoming. If you weren't growing, you wouldn't be here. You would have turned away by now.

This isn't a repeat. It's a reckoning. You're not back at the beginning; you've returned to the edge. That's the difference. This time you have awareness. You have enough history with yourself to know the difference between who you were and who you're willing to be. Now let the mirror show you, not to measure progress but to remind you that you're not starting over. You're starting from where you actually are, and that's more than enough.

RECURRENCE AS COMMITMENT

Who you are is *what* you return to. You're not becoming *who* you intend to be. You're becoming *what* you consistently return

THE RECURRENCE EFFECT

to every day in a thousand small moments—without announcements, without fanfare. You are remaking yourself. The question isn't "Are you growing?" It's "What are you returning to?" This isn't about chasing a breakthrough. It's about sticking with the beat and letting go of the obsession around outcomes. You don't become by hitting goals. You become by returning to what matters—especially when no one's keeping score. Progress isn't the prize; presence is. If you can stay with the process—even when it's boring, even when it's slow—you just might become someone your goals could never predict.

Recurrence is not a loop. It's a declaration. Recurrence isn't a cycle of failure. It's a statement of priority. Every time you come back to something—a pattern of belief or a posture—you reinforce it. You give it shape, and you give it power. You may not mean to, but your rhythm doesn't lie. That's why recurrence is sacred. It doesn't espouse your goals; it exposes your truth.

The mirror isn't asking for change. It's asking for clarity. That is where the Learning Knowing Mirror shows up, not as an interrogation but as a ritual, a quiet return, and a pulse check. It doesn't demand transformation. It asks only this: "What still matters, what no longer serves, what have you outgrown?" It asks it every time you return, not to punish you but to anchor you in the present—not in memory, not in aspiration, but in what's alive right now.

Return isn't repeating. It's revealing. You think you're just circling back, but the way you return—the how, the why—is the shape of your becoming. Whether you realize it or not, your rhythm is making a claim on your values, your identity, and your integrity. That's why recurrence is not just a pattern; it's a commitment to what you keep choosing, even when no one's watching.

NO ONE GROWS IN STRAIGHT LINES

RETURN FROM THE DRIFT

What you return to, you endorse. It's time to stop talking about what you believe and start asking what you're loyal to—not once but every time. You endorse what you protect and reinforce, and what you return to, you become.

◉ AWAKEN

- What am I still repeating that no longer reflects who I'm becoming?
- If I had to live this rhythm again and again, exactly as it is, what would I finally change for?

◉ REMEMBER

- What I return to—not what I hope for—reveals who I'm becoming.
- The mirror reflects my pattern, not my potential.

↩ RETURN

- What one action today can declare this is done?
- What rhythm do I need to let go of—not because it's bad but because I've outgrown it?

This isn't the end of reflection. It's what you do with what you saw. This is where people like to check out and say they've done the inner work to label the insight and move on. But if that's all you do, you've missed the purpose. Evaluation doesn't give you a clean slate. It gives you a mirror, and now that you've seen what's in it, you're responsible for it.

Reflection doesn't conclude; it commits. You've seen the difference between what you believe and how you behave. You've noticed the rhythm. You've watched the spiral, and now it's not about what you saw. It's about what you'll stand for, what you'll stop excusing, what you'll refuse to carry forward unconsciously. This is the threshold between observation and authorship.

The mirror doesn't close the chapter; it sets the standard. The mirror doesn't say you're finished. It asks, "Are you still there? Are you still aligned? Are you still honest?" From this moment forward, you're measured not by what you see but by what you return to when no one's looking.

Alignment isn't a feeling. It's a fierce daily choice. So here's what we do next. You've seen it. You've felt it. You've faced it. Now comes the daily act of courage to live it. The next step isn't about clarity; it's about congruence—not what you know but what you practice in your choices, in your tone, in your timing, and in your willingness to stay real when performance would be easier. Alignment isn't a destination. It's a rhythm that starts the moment you stop just seeing clearly and start living honestly.

Knowing it isn't enough. Now you choose. You've seen the truth—not the polished version but the one that lingers. You've watched yourself spiral, stretch, and fracture. You've stood in the discomfort. You've returned not just once but on purpose. That's growth. But it's not the end. It's the edge, and now the question is simple and somewhat brutal. Will you live what you saw—not when it's easy but when it costs you?

Theologian and philosopher Augustine of Hippo is believed to have said, "Hope has two beautiful daughters; their names are Anger and Courage. Anger at the way things are, and Courage to see that they do not remain as they are." If what you saw in the mirror stirred some anger, that's good. That means you're awake. But anger without courage just becomes complaint—numbing disguised as a passion. Hope is only real if it moves, and the only thing strong enough to move you now is courage—not once but every day.

Alignment isn't principle; it's practice. The next chapter is about whether your actions can hold the weight of your awareness and whether your values are visible when things get inconvenient. Alignment doesn't show up when you're feeling inspired. It must show up when you're under pressure, in conflict, and alone. That is where growth gets real, not as insight but as integrity.

The daily test starts now—no new insight, no shiny framework, just the most relentless question you can ask yourself: "Am I living in alignment right now?" Then ask it again and again and again. Here's where you need both of hope's daughters. You need anger at what's no longer acceptable, and you need courage to live in alignment and return every day. This isn't a performance. It's not a vow. It's devotion to a rhythm.

CHAPTER 9

ALIGNMENT IS A DAILY ACT OF COURAGE

Vision is not enough, it must be combined with venture. It is not enough to stare up the steps, we must step up the stairs.

VÁCLAV HAVEL

Alignment takes more than awareness. Knowing isn't the hardest part. Living is. Alignment is a repeated, often invisible practice. You've looked in the mirror. You've seen the cracks. You've named the tension. You've stood in front of the truth, and for a moment you've stopped pretending that's progress. But let's not lie to ourselves. Awareness isn't transformation. It's not even momentum.

THE RECURRENCE EFFECT

You're not stuck because you don't know what matters. You're stuck because it's dangerous and scary to live like it does.

We want alignment to be clean like a goal we can set or a statement we can make. But alignment isn't declared. It's demonstrated not once but in rhythm—every meeting, every boundary, every hard no, every awkward yes. It's not a destination where you finally arrive. It's a friction-filled practice you return to every time. Life gives you the opportunity to forget what you saw in the mirror.

Alignment isn't inspiration; it's integrity. And integrity isn't about being good. It's about being honest—honest about who you're trying to become; honest about how you keep drifting; and honest enough to stop outsourcing the problem to your schedule, your stress, or your team.

Here's the question: If I watched your day, just any ordinary Tuesday, would I see what you say you believe, or would I see the performance you've polished to avoid the cost? Alignment doesn't happen in big moments. There are no grand gestures. It happens in dozens of small ones that no one celebrates and that you'll have to repeat tomorrow.

The mirror is only the beginning. At the end of the previous chapter, you stood with a mirror in your hand, not to admire yourself but to confront the truth. Now you find out what it's really for. The mirror shows you the gap between knowing and doing, but it doesn't close the gap for you. That part's on you. That's where alignment begins, where the image of who you imagine yourself to be meets the reality of who you are. It's like business coach and entrepreneur Dan Sullivan said, "Someone once told me the definition of Hell: The last day you have on earth, the person you became will meet the person you could have become."

ALIGNMENT IS A DAILY ACT OF COURAGE

The gap is the moment you see what matters but still hesitate to protect it. It's the moment you say "I don't have time" when the truth is "I'm not ready to pay the price." But the Learning Knowing Mirror is not there to motivate you. It's there to interrupt you, to show you the places where your calendar, your tone, and your follow-through are betraying what you claim to value.

If you can hold that discomfort without flinching, that's the beginning of real alignment. It's easy to name your values or talk about what matters. It's another thing entirely to incarnate those values, to give them shape in your posture, your timing, and your tone. That's the work. That's the practice. You don't find alignment. You forge it moment by moment when no one's watching.

Let's be honest. Most of us are addicted to understanding. We consume content. We attend training. We take notes. We tell ourselves we're growing because we're learning, but learning is not the same as evolving. The truth is, you don't change through comprehension. You change through commitment when your body follows what your mind already knows. That is why so many people stall here. They confuse clarity for courage.

Clarity is clean. Courage is messy. Clarity feels good. Courage rarely does. There's no applause for the first time you say no to something that used to define you. There's no spotlight when you speak the truth that might cost you comfort, and yet *that's* where the shift happens—not in your beliefs but in your behaviors.

Former British Prime Minister Benjamin Disraeli said, "Action may not always bring happiness; but there is no happiness without action." This quote isn't about chasing joy. It's about refusing to be adrift. It's about how doing—even awkward, incomplete, imperfect doing—is the only path to alignment that lasts. You don't feel your way into integrity. You act your way there, one choice at a time, one moment of courage at a time. Every time you do, something shifts, not in the world but inside you.

You're already on the hook. You already saw it. The moment you noticed the dissonance, you became responsible for it. You don't get to unsee what you've seen. You cannot pretend you don't know anymore, and that's not punishment. It's an invitation. Alignment is not some distant peak you conquer. It's rhythm, a ritual, and a return every time you choose presence over performance—every time you stop seeking clarity and start practicing congruence; every time you stop pretending you don't know better and finally act like you do. That's not perfection or arrival; it's alignment. It is not fun or happy, but it is real.

Alignment is a daily act of courage, especially when it costs you, especially when it's quiet, and especially when no one else sees. This isn't about *learning* anymore; it's about *living*. Now we enter the place where alignment becomes reality—in the small, sacred, inconvenient choices you make every single day.

THE WEIGHT OF SMALL CHOICES

We all love the mythology of the big moment, the dramatic leap, the pivot, the burn-it-down decision, and the day everything changes. But your life is not shaped by those moments. It's shaped by what you repeat when no one's paying attention—by how you respond when nothing big is at stake, just your character. It's shaped in the hallway conversations, the rushed emails, the small justifications, the tone you use when you're tired, the habit you defend when it's convenient.

The hardest part is that those moments don't *feel* important. They feel forgettable and routine like background noise, but they're

ALIGNMENT IS A DAILY ACT OF COURAGE

not. They are the terrain of your actual alignment, and they shape who you're becoming, whether you're conscious of it or not.

Alignment hides in the ordinary, and that's why we miss it. We live in a world obsessed with spectacle. We look for meaning in the massive, but alignment shows up in what you think doesn't matter. It's the second glance you give your phone instead of your partner. It's the email you never answer. It's the pause you ignore. It's the meeting where you nod along instead of speaking up. It's the meeting where somebody says something, and you notice the tone—you know there's more there but you just blow by it because you don't want to open up that can of worms.

These are the things that build you, not because they're loud but because they're repeated. What you repeat is what you become. We want to believe that we're shaped by our intentions, that our internal declarations count for more than our lived rhythm. But your rhythm is the real you. Your repetition is your truth.

You might say you're committed to honesty, but if your daily habits protect comfort over confrontation, that's the real story. You might say you value presence, but if you're multitasking your way through every conversation, your nervous system is writing a different narrative. We tell ourselves the small things don't matter because we're afraid to confront how consistently we compromise what we say we value. But the ordinary isn't neutral. It's sacred, and the way you treat it, the way you inhabit the invisible, is where your alignment either grows or erodes.

Real alignment is quietly disruptive and costly. Let's go deeper into that cost because we're not just talking about small choices; we're talking about what it costs to keep making them in a world that rewards compromise. Real alignment doesn't make you more agreeable. It makes you more honest, which means it's going to get uncomfortable fast.

THE RECURRENCE EFFECT

The moment you start living in rhythm with what you know is true is when you begin threatening the systems, relationships, and stories that are benefiting from your drift. It's that friend who liked you better when you didn't have boundaries. It's the client who preferred you when you were always available. It's that inner voice that tells you to stay quiet and avoid making waves. All of those will push back, and you will have to decide every day, "Do I live aligned, or do I go back to being digestible for others?"

Alignment is not about moral high ground. It's about existential friction—the way your truth grinds against other people's expectations. It's the seductive returning to the version of you that was easier to manage. That's why most people don't lose their integrity in one massive betrayal. It erodes in tiny concessions, smiling when you should speak, agreeing when you mean no, staying when everything in you says go. That's the slow rot of misalignment. It feels easier in the short term, but the longer you avoid disruption on the outside, the more violence you commit on the inside.

Meaning and courage live in the micro, and they always have. You do not need a breakthrough, a mountaintop, or a permission slip to start living in alignment. You don't. You just need to wake up to the moments you've been dismissing because those are the ones that shape you. It's not the career shift, the new city, or the applause-worthy move. It's the moment you choose honesty when it would be easier to lie, the moment you show up late and choose not to explain yourself, the moment you don't check your phone, or the moment you pause before reacting.

These are not warm-ups for the real thing. These *are* the real things. You are made in the micro, and the micro is where your courage is constantly being tested. Here is one of my favorite quotes from Mother Teresa: "There are no great things, only small things with great love. Happy are those." This isn't sentimental; it's structural. It reminds us that meaning is made through devotion, not drama, and that you don't need to wait for your life to become extraordinary. You need to show up fully to the ordinary you already have.

Who you are is what you repeat. You don't rise to the level of your values. You return to the level of your rhythm—not what you hope for, not what you post about, not what you aspire to, but what you do when it's hard, when no one sees, and when it costs you. That's the pattern that forms you, and it's the pattern you either choose or unconsciously obey.

Ask yourself what your small choices protect. What do they reveal about what you truly value? You are not what you believe. You are what you repeat. You are what you choose when nothing big is on the line. You are what you return to when the world stops watching because now you've seen the cost of alignment in the mundane. If you're willing to face that, then you're ready for what comes next—the cost of holding integrity in a world that benefits from your drift.

THE COST OF INTEGRITY

Integrity isn't free. There's a cost to becoming that's not a metaphor or a concept but a real, felt cost. Alignment sounds good until you realize that it asks you to leave something behind. The longer you've carried it, the more it's wrapped itself around your identity. That's why most people never step into integrity, not fully, because somewhere deep down they already know it's going to hurt. It will require shedding silence, being misunderstood, and worst of all, rebuilding how you relate to yourself.

THE RECURRENCE EFFECT

People perform alignment because truly living it feels unsafe. This isn't about weakness; it's about rewiring. Your nervous system was built to avoid threat, not to seek truth. The moment you challenge the roles, rhythms, and routines that have kept you safe, your brain doesn't think you're evolving. It says you are in danger. So most people do what society readily expects and accepts from them. They talk about boundaries, but they don't hold them. They proclaim values but compromise under pressure. They posture as being evolved but return to old defaults the moment it gets uncomfortable.

Why? Because certainty *feels* like control, and control *feels* like survival. That's what the Learning Knowing Mirror reveals—not just a gap between what you say and what you do, but the reason for the gap. Certainty is a dopamine hit. It calms the amygdala. It rewards performance even when it's fake.[57]

Real growth triggers a ton of anxiety. It exposes dissonance. It stretches identity. When the mirror says you *know* better but you're not *doing* better, it is really asking, "Are you willing to feel unsafe for the sake of your integrity?" And for many people, the answer is no. They rationalize delay, they spin a better story, and they slowly and quietly settle.

Let me be absolutely clear about this and all other points I am making. There is absolutely no judgment associated with these ideas as long as you *own the choice*. Everyone is free to choose, but you must accept the existence of the choice and not act in bad faith. As Jeanne-Paul Sartre said, "What is not possible is not to choose. I can always choose, but if I do not choose, I am still choosing."[58]

Integrity always demands a reckoning with what you built while you were asleep. Here's the existential rupture most people avoid: "What if the life I built was designed to protect the version

ALIGNMENT IS A DAILY ACT OF COURAGE

of me I no longer want to be?" That's what alignment threatens—not just your schedule but your sense of self.

It begins small. You can't sit through the same meetings. You notice how often you soften your voice to avoid conflict. You look at your calendar and wonder, "Who is this even for?" Then it hits your body. You dread conversations you used to tolerate. Your chest tightens when you say yes too quickly. You feel nauseous after small talk that goes nowhere. This is the body becoming honest before your mind catches up. The body doesn't care about stories. It lives truth in real time, and what it starts telling you is that you are out of rhythm.

What used to work now makes you sick. What used to feel like success now feels like betrayal. The worst part is that you can't unsee it. Once the Learning Knowing Mirror is activated, it doesn't stop reflecting. It keeps asking, "What are you still tolerating? What no longer honors your evolution? What commitments are you clinging to out of fear, not fidelity?" And once you name them, you're faced with the real cost. You can't live in alignment and keep your old self intact. Integrity means burning what no longer fits—not because it was wrong but because it's no longer yours.

Integrity means being misunderstood by those who benefited from your compromise. There's a myth we need to dismantle that once you get clear and aligned, people will celebrate you. They won't because the moment you stop playing the role they wrote for you, you disrupt the script. They like the agreeable version of you, the self-sacrificing one, the one who didn't ask for much.

When you change your rhythm, when you start moving to your own beat, they say you're selfish, confusing, or not the same, and they're right. As Frederich Nietzsche said, "And those who were seen dancing were thought to be insane by those who could not hear the music."

THE RECURRENCE EFFECT

That is where loneliness sets in. The path of integrity is a narrow one, not because you're superior but because you're no longer available to stay connected on someone else's terms. You stop explaining and stop apologizing or trying to manage other people's discomfort with your growth. In that silence, you remember your own rhythm—the one you abandoned when you started people-pleasing, the one you silenced to stay safe, the one you compromised to avoid being alone.

But here's the truth. Once you hear it again, you can't go back. You can't pretend you're okay shrinking. You can't pretend you don't know. You can't pretend performance is enough because the cost of pretending becomes too high.

Integrity is a threshold where you choose truth over belonging. You don't get to keep everything, not if you want to stay honest. Some relationships will dissolve. Some rules will no longer fit. Some stories will start to rot in your mouth the moment you try to speak them. That's not failure. That's the price of returning to yourself.

REFLECTION PAUSE

When the mirror asks, "What do you know that you're not living?" it's not trying to guilt you. It's offering you a door, but you can't walk through it carrying everything. You'll have to set some things down—certainty, approval, control, the need to be understood. Integrity doesn't promise comfort. It promises congruence, not a happy ending but a faithful return to what you already knew and to who you were before you learned to perform. The silence that comes after integrity is painful, but it's also holy. What comes next is uncertainty and the commitment to act even when you don't feel ready.

ALIGNMENT IS A DAILY ACT OF COURAGE

👁 AWAKEN

- Where in your life are you performing instead of practicing?
- What's the story you're telling yourself to justify the misalignment?

📍 REMEMBER

- Integrity isn't loud. It's quiet, repeated, and often inconvenient.
- The fastest way to lose yourself is by making someone else comfortable.

↩ RETURN

- What's one commitment you've outgrown but keep honoring out of fear?
- What's the smallest possible act of alignment you can take today, even if no one sees it?

CONSISTENCY WITHOUT CERTAINTY

Clarity isn't a prerequisite for alignment. We've been taught to wait until we're sure, until the timing is right, until the noise dies down, or until we feel ready. But alignment doesn't wait. It asks, "What will you return to even when the path ahead is fogged with doubt?" The truth is that you don't get clarity first. You get practice. You get friction. You get movement. If you stay long enough, you get rhythm. Staying takes courage—not the loud kind, not the heroic kind, but the original kind. The word *courage* comes from the Latin *cor*, meaning "heart."[59] Its earliest meaning

THE RECURRENCE EFFECT

was telling the story of who you are with your whole heart, even when your voice shakes.

Alignment doesn't begin with clarity. It begins with the willingness to act before you feel ready. To live what matters without proof, without applause, and without guarantees isn't confidence. That's courage in its oldest form.

As we've discussed, your brain treats uncertainty as a threat. It's a function of evolutionary biology. Our brains weren't built for alignment. They were built for survival and keeping us safe.

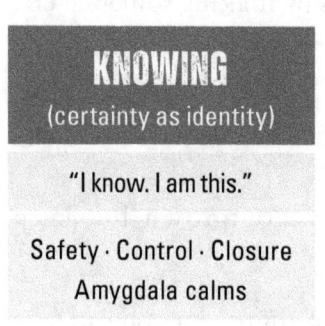

According to the Learning Knowing Mirror, the first stage most of us live in is Knowing and Certainty as Identity where "I know" becomes "I am this."

Why do we cling so tightly to certainty and knowing? It's because certainty calms the amygdala. It soothes the nervous system. It tells your body you're safe now that you have this figured out. When you're confronted with ambiguity—when your values ask you to act before you're sure—your threat-detection system lights up, your heart rate increases, and your body wants to get out of that situation. Research backs this up.

The ventral striatum, your brain's reward center, lights up when things feel resolved. Even when it's wrong, certainty gives us a dopamine hit.[60] That's why being right feels good even when it blocks our growth. When we say "consistency without certainty," we're not just asking you to do something hard. We're asking you to override your own wiring—to move while your body is screaming "Stop! Wait! Be sure!" That's not just discipline. That's courage in motion. Courage isn't the absence of fear; it's the decision to act without guarantees.

ALIGNMENT IS A DAILY ACT OF COURAGE

The Learning Knowing Mirror shows a pivotal shift from Cognitive Dissonance (something doesn't add up) to Emerging Awareness (maybe I was wrong). This is the most vulnerable stage because you're between identities. You've outgrown the old one, but the new one hasn't taken shape yet. Here is where most people flinch because the old certainty is gone and the new pattern isn't stable yet.

This is where the practice of alignment begins—not with confidence and not with clarity but with a quiet, persistent return to what you know is true, even if you don't feel it yet. Returning without applause or reinforcement requires more than resolve; it requires courage—the kind you can't outsource and no one else can model for you. You act in alignment *before* it feels natural. You choose what matters *before* it makes sense to anyone else. You show up differently *before* you have the words to explain why. This isn't inspirational; it's uncomfortable.

If you can hold your posture through the discomfort, you enter the next stage of the mirror, which is Learning—I am always becoming—where neuroplasticity kicks in. That is where patterns start to shift; where consistency rewires your identity; and where slowly over time, the alignment that once felt foreign becomes familiar.[61] It's not because you became certain but because you stayed courageous when it would have been easier to retreat.

Certainty is the island. Alignment is the wave. The island feels safe, stable, and stagnant. Alignment—the wave—is moving, alive, and uncertain. The island tells you, "Just wait here. Eventually things will make sense." But as Henry David Thoreau said, "You must live in the present, launch yourself on every wave, find your eternity in each moment. Fools stand on their islands of opportunities and look toward another island. There is no other land; there is no other life but this."[62] Thoreau wasn't being poetic. He was

THE RECURRENCE EFFECT

calling you out because the life you want isn't on another island. It's in the ocean, in the wave, in the risk, in the now.

You don't get alignment by calculating the odds. You get it by leaping, even when your old self begs you to stay still. Consistency without certainty is not about being brave *once*. It's about being brave again tomorrow, again the day after that, and again the day after that. Courage doesn't just show up in grand decisions. It lives in the choice to keep moving with no applause, no guarantee, and no clarity—only a rhythm, only a knowing that this is the direction your body refuses to betray anymore.

The goal isn't to feel ready. It's to move anyway. The goal isn't to feel certain. It's to show up again, even in the fog. The mirror isn't asking, "Are you clear?" It's asking, "Are you congruent in motion? Are your choices reflecting what matters even when you're unsure?" The more you answer yes—not once but repeatedly—the more your nervous system adapts, the more your rhythm returns, and the more your alignment becomes a lived pattern, not a forced performance.

You didn't find your way by being certain. You found it by staying courageous long enough to let the rhythm take hold. This isn't about being sure. It's about having the heart to act without certainty, to return without proof, and to live as if your choices matter—because they do.

Remember, the root of courage isn't strength. It begins with heart and the willingness to live open even when everything inside you wants to close, because the next wave is already rising. The moment you leap again, especially when you're unsure, you become more aligned than most people ever let themselves be—not perfect but present and faithful.

ALIGNMENT IS A DAILY ACT OF COURAGE

THE RITUALS OF REALIGNMENT

Repetition isn't failure; it's a form of fate. Let's talk about the moments you come back to—not the big decisions but the quiet ones, the ones that don't announce themselves. Realignment doesn't happen in breakthroughs; it happens in returns—not the dramatic kind but the kind that whispers, "You drifted; come back" over and over again. You're not becoming who you *intend* to be. You're becoming what you *return* to. That's not weakness; that's rhythm, and rhythm is how transformation actually lives.

You don't need more resolve. You need a ritual. Most people think they're inconsistent because they lack willpower, but willpower isn't the problem. Friction is. In a world wired for drift, the cost of return gets higher every time. When you forget where the center is, you need a ritual—not another burst of motivation, not another plan, and not a routine. You need a ritual—a sacred repetition, a recurring anchor, a quiet question you ask yourself, something that calls you home.

The Learning Knowing Mirror reflects that moment of return. It doesn't measure your beliefs. It reveals the behavioral fidelity that you actually practice when the clarity fades. Think about where you are in the mirror. Maybe you're in Emerging Awareness where you say, "Maybe I was wrong." Or maybe you're in Learning where "I'm always becoming."

Either way, the mirror is asking you the same thing: "Will you return again without guarantees?" Rituals are not tools of certainty. They're acts of devotion, and devotion doesn't promise clarity. It only promises proximity to yourself, to the truth, and to the next honest choice.

Return is a phenomenological event. You meet yourself in time. Return isn't just behavior; it's being in the world. When

THE RECURRENCE EFFECT

you come back to a ritual, you don't just repeat an action. You reencounter yourself in time. You pause. You feel. You ask, "Is this still true? Is this still mine?" That is what separates ritual from routine.

Routine reinforces function. Ritual reveals form—the shape you are becoming. Phenomenologically, it's the moment when time is no longer abstract. It's lived, felt, and thick. You realize that every repetition is a claim, not about who you are but about who you're willing to be. Each return becomes an existential checkpoint. Are you still aligned with your deeper becoming, or are you just maintaining what feels familiar? That is why courage matters. Most people don't avoid rituals out of laziness. They avoid them because they know if they pause long enough, they'll have to tell the truth without performance. That's courage.

You don't become yourself in theory. You become yourself in rhythm. Irvin Yalom wrote, "The spirit of a man is constructed out of his choices"[63]—not his thoughts, not his beliefs, not his intentions, but his choices. This isn't motivational language. It's existential architecture because in the existential tradition, your identity is not found; it's authored.

You are what you *choose*, especially when the choice is repeated, embodied, and made without the assurance of success. That is why ritual matters. Every time you return to the same hard yes, every time you choose integrity over convenience, and every time you say no to what no longer fits, you are building something—something stable enough to hold meaning; something strong enough to survive uncertainty; and something resilient enough to outlast your mood, your doubts, and your distractions.

That is also why the Learning Knowing Mirror doesn't ask, "What do you believe?" It asks, "What are you repeating? What do your rhythms protect? What choices shape your days and, by

ALIGNMENT IS A DAILY ACT OF COURAGE

extension, your becoming?" Existentially speaking, the choices you ritualize are the self you return to.

Returning isn't control. It's commitment. We don't use rituals to stay in control. We use them to stay in relationship with our values, our direction, and our evolution. Rituals aren't about discipline. They're about commitment to who you're willing to become—one repeated choice at a time. Return is so uncomfortable because every return is a reckoning: "Is the version of me I'm living still worthy of the person I'm becoming?"

Courage isn't loud here. It's quiet, repetitive, and unseen. But that's the kind that matters most. When the noise comes (and it will) and when the old rhythms try to pull you back (and they will), you need something stronger than willpower. You need a rhythm worth returning to—something personal, something embodied. It's not a command but a cue, a phrase, a space, a scent, a note, or a breath. You need something that says, "Come back; begin again," and you will again and again.

As you do, you'll shape the kind of person who can face the next threshold. What comes next isn't more repetition. It's refinement—not just staying in rhythm but deciding what no longer belongs in the pattern at all—not because you're sure but because you're still here and because you've built a rhythm strong enough to return to.

Soon we'll learn what must be released so what remains is not just consistent but true.

WHAT YOU'RE WILLING TO LOSE

What are you willing to lose—not hypothetically, not conceptually, but really? Alignment isn't a concept. It's a cut. You don't just declare what matters and walk forward untouched. You leave things behind: people, roles, scripts, and versions of yourself that once kept you safe, admired, and accepted. This is the moment that separates *knowing* from *becoming*. Many people don't make it—not because they're weak but because the price of becoming feels too much like dying.

You can't align with the future while clinging to the past. You can't bring everything with you. You can't stay loyal to your past and live in integrity with your future. Something has to break because alignment isn't additive; it's subtractive. It clears. It strips. It empties. The deeper you've gone in this process, the more you've reflected, returned, and reevaluated; the more clearly the misalignments show up in your calendar, your conversations, and your compliance.

The Learning Knowing Mirror doesn't soften the blow. It confronts you. *You know this isn't true anymore. You keep showing up for something you've already outgrown. You're clinging to comfort while claiming to have clarity.* This is the crisis of congruence—the moment that awareness is no longer the work.

Letting go is an existential act of self-authorship. Phenomenologically, who you are is not fixed. You are not a role. You are not your habits. You are not what others expect of you. You are not a human being; you are a human *becoming*, and becoming requires loss. That is what people misunderstand about alignment. They think it's addition, refinement, and polish, but it's actually about subtraction—not just surface-level shedding but the deep work of confronting what identities were inherited, not chosen.

What relationships are being preserved at the expense of your integrity? What part of you still needs to be seen as good, stable, or certain even when that version is no longer real? Letting go isn't a strategy. It's grief—and grief, as the existentialists remind us, is the price of meaning. If it didn't matter, it wouldn't hurt to release it. But you can't carry what's next if your hands are full of what no longer belongs.

Knowing isn't enough. You have to move. At this stage, it's easy to stall, to stand in what you've seen, to analyze it, to name it, to understand it. But knowing isn't movement. Reflection isn't refinement.

That is why I began this chapter with the words of playwright, dissident, and former Czech President Václav Havel, who said. "Vision is not enough, it must be combined with venture. It is not enough to stare up the steps, we must step up the stairs." That's the difference between intention and alignment. One is theoretical; the other is embodied. The quote reminds us that transformation isn't just about insight or clarity. It's about the courage to act without a guarantee, to move while still uncertain, and to carry the weight of your values even when the climb gets steep.

The stairs won't ascend for you. You have to take each one breath by breath and step by step, knowing that you might stumble but trusting that embodiment matters more than polish.

That is what distinguishes alignment from performance. Alignment costs you something. It's not an idea you hold; it's a rhythm you return to. And every step you take isn't just movement; it's authorship.

This loss is what most people delay because it requires not just action but release. You don't just move forward. You walk away from what was familiar, from what worked, from what earned you validation and comfort and praise but no longer tells the truth. That's what makes it courageous because you'll feel the cost. In the empty space that follows, you create room for someone new, someone quieter, someone truer, and someone less bound by what they were and more devoted to what they're becoming.

Letting go isn't loss for its own sake. It's clearing the way for who you're becoming. You're not shedding for the sake of loss. You're creating space for the next version of you to emerge. That version won't be born of more thinking, more vision boards, or more frameworks. It will be born through what you're willing to walk away from without certainty, without applause, and without needing to explain.

This is courage: not a feeling but a choice; not once but every day. You've come this far. You've told the truth. You've returned over and over, and now you let go, not because it's easy but because it's time. It's time to stop carrying what was never yours. It's time to loosen your grip on what once served but now suffocates. It's time to move forward lighter. It's not to move faster but to move more freely.

RETURN FROM THE DRIFT

What's next isn't just movement. It's refinement, and refinement isn't just knowing what to add. It's finally being willing to cut what doesn't belong. The only way to begin is by choosing what you're willing to leave behind.

👁 AWAKEN

- When was the last time you felt completely at peace with how you're living?
- What happens in your body when you know you're out of alignment?

ALIGNMENT IS A DAILY ACT OF COURAGE

📍 REMEMBER

- Alignment isn't a destination. It's a rhythm you return to.
- Courage lives in the choice to act without applause.

↩ RETURN

- What simple ritual could you use to realign when you drift?
- How will you remind yourself to return again and again when the world pulls you away?

You've looked in the mirror. You've named what no longer fits. You've seen where you've drifted. You've told the truth, maybe for the first time in years, but the reflection is not the finish line. It's the Forge. Truth isn't enough if you won't carry it. The real question is this: "Will you carry what you've seen into the way you live, and will you carry it not once, not only when it's easy, but again and again?"

Alignment isn't an event; it's a pattern of return. You don't align once and move on. You align and return. You align and adjust. You align and edit. Some days you don't feel like you're making progress. You feel messy, fractured, and unsure. That's normal because alignment isn't about being flawless. It's about being faithful to what you now see, to what you now know, and to the rhythm that has finally begun to speak more clearly than the noise.

The Learning Knowing Mirror taught us that clarity doesn't matter if you refuse to act on it. Awareness without alignment is just more performance. But rhythm, real rhythm, is built through embodied decisions over time.

You're not moving forward. You're moving deeper. What's ahead of you isn't a staircase. It's a descent, a refinement, a narrowing of what you carry and who you choose to be. That's the shift we're in now, from Evaluation to Editing, from truth-telling to truth-editing. The mess you've uncovered wasn't a detour. It was preparation.

Alignment showed you what doesn't fit. Now comes the work of choosing what you'll release and what you'll build from what remains. As you do, something begins to lift, not because the journey is over but because you're no longer dragging what was never yours. You've become lighter but not weightless. What remains after letting go is what matters most, and what matters most always carries weight—fewer commitments but deeper ones; fewer beliefs but ones you're willing to embody.

German philosopher G. W. F. Hegel wrote, "The length of the journey has to be borne with, for every moment is necessary."[64] That includes the spirals, the stalling, the parts where nothing made sense. You weren't stuck. You were being shaped, and now you're ready to cut. You're ready to Edit.

This isn't resolution. This is the edge, the boundary between seeing and becoming. You don't cross with certainty. You cross with courage, the courage to say, "This is done. This no longer belongs. I am no longer available for who I used to be." That's because your identity is not a *fact*. It's a *draft*. What you do next, how you move, what you carry, what you Edit—that's the first sentence of the next version of you.

You've stood in front of the mirror. You've told the truth. You've returned. You've released. Now it's time to shape the life that can hold what matters, not with more information, not with more performance, but with fewer and truer commitments. Becoming isn't about adding more. It's about choosing what you're finally ready to carry, what you're willing to leave behind, and what you are willing to Edit.

PART IV
EDIT
(WITH CONVICTION)

CHAPTER 10

YOUR IDENTITY ISN'T A FACT; IT'S A DRAFT

Human beings are works in progress that mistakenly think they're finished.

DANIEL GILBERT

You've told the truth. You've named the drift. You've stood in front of the mirror and seen what no longer fits. Now comes the part that most people avoid. You must Edit—cut. This is the moment when alignment becomes authorship, when knowing becomes choosing, and when intention becomes incision, because clarity isn't the hard part.

Editing is living. What matters means letting go of what doesn't—and not just habits but identities, roles, and stories that once kept you safe, liked, and accepted. Editing isn't about becoming someone new. It's about becoming more fully yourself by conscious choice. It's not self-improvement but rather self-authorship, and authorship starts here, not with vision but with a blade. Albert Camus explained it like this:

> Get scared. It will do you good. Smoke a bit, stare blankly at some ceilings, beat your head against some walls, refuse to see some people, paint and write. Get scared some more. Allow your little mind to do nothing but function. Stay inside, go out—I don't care what you'll do; but stay scared as hell. You will never be able to experience everything. So, please, do poetical justice to your soul and simply experience yourself.[65]

This isn't a motivational quote; it's an invitation to confrontation. Camus isn't glorifying fear. He's reminding us that fear is evidence that you're getting close to the truth, that to experience yourself—to do poetic justice to your soul—you will have to feel what most people try to numb such as discomfort, grief, dissonance, and desire. That's what Editing demands.

You can't experience everything, but you can experience yourself now. It's not the persona or the performance but the raw, real, unfinished you—the one you've kept buried under old stories, expectations, and roles you've outgrown. To meet that version of yourself, you'll have to Edit—you'll have to cut.

The mirror for this section is the Conscious Cut. Like each of the mirrors we've used, it is not here to flatter you. It doesn't offer clarity; it demands consequence. It's called the Conscious Cut because every decision you make here is a vote for the self you're becoming. This isn't passive reflection. This is ruthless discernment.

YOUR IDENTITY ISN'T A FACT; IT'S A DRAFT

No cut you make is random. It's filtered by tension, truth, and what you're finally willing to face. You decide what needs to be cut by answering filtering questions, such as these:

- Am I choosing clarity?
- Am I living from agency or still appeasing for approval?
- Are my rhythms aligned with who I'm becoming, or are they just familiar?

THE CONSCIOUS CUT MIRROR

FILTER	CORE TENSION	GUIDING QUESTIONS	SIGNAL TO CUT	SIGNAL TO KEEP
CLARITY > COMFORT	Truth vs. safety	Is this clear or just comfortable? Would I still choose this if I wasn't afraid?	Instant relief, rationalization, numbing	Discomfort with integrity, honest tension
COST = COMMITMENT	Change vs. convenience	What am I giving up to grow? Where am I faking the cost of becoming?	No loss, no disruption, performance-only	Real friction, identity tension, investment
WORTH RETURNING TO	Pattern vs. impulse	Would I be proud to repeat this choice? Is this building a rhythm I respect?	Regret, resentment, "just this once"	Micro-integrity, small actions with soul
AGENCY > APPROVAL	Authorship vs. appeasement	Who am I performing for? What if no one claps?	Seeking validation, hiding truth, emotional editing	Coherence, ownership, action without audience
ALIGNMENT > ACHIEVEMENT	Coherence vs. success	Does this reflect who I'm becoming? What am I achieving at the cost of my soul?	Burnout, emptiness, self-betrayal	Grounded impact, deep satisfaction, quiet power

THE RECURRENCE EFFECT

Use these filters as thresholds when you're facing a choice, a shift, or a moment of doubt. They won't give you answers. They'll cut out the garbage and reveal what's real. Before—or after—a decision, consider these questions to figure out where you may be drifting. You could also use the filters here proactively. Highlight one each week to observe how it shows up in your life. Practice returning to the signals. Your body often knows what's happening before your mind admits it.

The first filter of the Conscious Cut mirror is Clarity > Comfort, which addresses the tension of truth versus safety. The clarity that truth brings is greater than the comfort of staying put where you feel safe. The questions here shed light on how fear of discomfort leads to drift:

- Is this clear or just comfortable?
- Would I still choose this if I wasn't afraid?

Pay close attention to how your body responds to the answers. These signals will tell you what to cut and what to keep. If you feel relief or numbness, or if you sense yourself rationalizing your choice, those are signals to cut. As counterintuitive as it may seem, feeling discomfort with integrity or an honest tension is a signal to keep going.

The second filter, Cost = Commitment, considers the tension of change versus convenience. Becoming costs you something, and that cost demonstrates your commitment to becoming. Here are the questions to decide what to cut and what to keep:

- What am I giving up to grow?
- Where am I faking the cost of becoming?

YOUR IDENTITY ISN'T A FACT; IT'S A DRAFT

When you make choices that cost you nothing, you won't feel any loss or disruption because you will be performing a convenient role. On the other hand, making choices that cost you something will feel like friction and tension between who you are and who you are becoming.

The third filter identifies pattern versus impulse. This is what the Worth Returning To filter asks:

- Would I be proud to repeat this choice?
- Is this building a rhythm I respect?

Your rhythm, what you return to again and again, should be consistent with what you want most and reinforce your becoming. The choices to keep will be small acts of integrity and soul. If your choices make you feel regret and resentment, it's clear what you should cut.

Agency > Approval is the fourth filter of the Conscious Cut Mirror. It reflects the tension of authorship versus appeasement. Choices that promote your agency and authorship in your becoming are greater than ones you make to appease others or gain their approval. Here are those questions:

- Who am I performing for?
- What if no one claps?

If the decisions you are considering are driven by a need for validation, a desire to hide the truth, or an inclination to bypass your emotions, those are the signals to cut. The signals to keep going with your decisions are internal coherence, a feeling of ownership in your actions, and the commitment to continue even when no one applauds.

THE RECURRENCE EFFECT

The Conscious Cut Mirror's final filter is Alignment > Achievement. That filter addresses the tension between being coherent and being successful. Alignment between your actions and your becoming is far greater than any external measure of success. Here are those questions:

- Does this reflect who I'm becoming?
- What am I achieving at the cost of my soul?

Chasing achievement will feel like burnout, emptiness, and self-betrayal, but alignment will make you feel deeply satisfied, grounded, and powerful.

The Conscious Cut is where you stop reacting and start revising. Not everything can come with you, and what you keep becomes your rhythm. Ask yourself, "What am I still performing that no longer belongs? What part of me is unfinished, not because I'm broken but because I haven't picked up the pen?" Editing is where you pick up the red pen, brandish it like a blade, and make the cut—not recklessly but consciously.

WHAT YOU CALL "YOU" IS JUST THE LATEST DRAFT

Every Edit is a vote for who you're becoming. Make it hurt a little. That's how you know it's real. And yes, it will hurt, but the pain of cutting is nothing compared to the cost of continuing to carry what was never truly yours. This isn't where you finish. This is where you finally begin.

You're not a fixed point. You're not a personality type. You're not the sum of your habits, your job title, or your Enneagram number. You're a draft. What you call "you" is just the latest

YOUR IDENTITY ISN'T A FACT; IT'S A DRAFT

version, the most recent Edit made by a thousand unseen forces—parents, teachers, trauma, praise, expectation, success. Some of it you choose; most of it you inherited.

One of the founders of humanistic psychology, American psychologist Carl Rogers, said, "A person is a fluid process, not a fixed and static entity; a flowing river of change, not a block of solid material; a continually changing constellation of potentialities, not a fixed quantity of traits."[66] If you've been treating your personality as a product, a fixed brand, or a defined identity, then it's no wonder you feel stuck. You were never meant to be static. You were meant to evolve consciously and intentionally. That's where the Conscious Cut comes in—not as a weapon but as a return to what's real, to what's yours.

Most of what we perform as identity is just a practice pattern reinforced by what has earned us praise, what has kept us safe, and what has earned us belonging in the past. Those patterns can't carry who you're becoming.

Every act of authorship starts with a cut. This isn't just reflection. This is revision. This is authorship. The cut might be small such as questioning a belief you've long defended, letting go of a role you no longer want to play, or refusing to soften your truth for the sake of being liked. Or it might be something seismic—ending something or saying no to something, finally being honest with someone or something. Either way, the question is the same: "Is this version of me designed for who I *was* or who I'm *becoming*?"

Organizational psychologist and author Benjamin Hardy reminds us that "personality isn't permanent."[67] Our personalities aren't permanent; they are echoes—a draft that feels like fact—because we've repeated something long enough to forget we're the ones who wrote it. The only thing that keeps it fixed is our avoidance of uncertainty.

THE RECURRENCE EFFECT

As Dr. Ellen Langer tells us, "If there are meaningful choices, there is uncertainty. If there is no choice, there is no uncertainty."[68] Hardy extends Langer's point and explains, "If you're unwilling to face and interact with uncertainty, then you've greatly limited who you are and what you've become. You've limited your ability to make choices, because all choices involve uncertainty and risk."[69] That's the tension of the Conscious Cut.

Every time you revise a story, you face risk. Every time you avoid it, you shrink your ability to choose. The choice is never between risk or safety. The choice is between becoming or repeating, and you can rest assured that it is disorienting. When you start cutting away the roles and beliefs that once worked—the high-performer, the fixer, the agreeable one—you'll feel raw.

Carl Rogers called this gap *incongruence*—the space between the ideal self, the version you think you should be, and the real self, the one you've buried under expectation and fear.[70] That's what you're reclaiming now—not a new self, just a more honest one. Let's be clear, you don't need to be polished; you need to be honest. You don't need to be certain. You need to choose because identity is not a fact; it's a draft. Right now you are holding the pen. So pick it up, make the Edit, and write what comes next, on purpose.

INHERITED SCRIPTS AND DEFAULT SETTINGS

You didn't write the first draft of yourself. You were born into a story already in motion—a family rhythm, a cultural script, a set of expectations—written long before you ever said your first word. Without realizing it, you internalized the rules. What gets rewarded, what gets ignored, what you need to feel safe, and

YOUR IDENTITY ISN'T A FACT; IT'S A DRAFT

what parts of you are too much are not enough. You learned how to survive, how to keep the peace, how to stay in the frame. Eventually you started calling this survival strategy your "self."

That didn't happen in a vacuum, as Albert Bandura's social learning theory shows.[71] We don't just become ourselves by experience. We become by observation. From the earliest moments, we were learning by watching how people around us behaved, what earned them praise, what got punished, whose voices were loudest, and whose voices were silenced. We observed what worked, and we adapted. We modeled ourselves on the roles that kept us included. We mirrored the behaviors that kept us safe. We reinforced what got results, and slowly and silently, those observations became identity—not chosen but absorbed; not authored but adopted.

You don't just carry your history. You carry the assumptions that are left behind. Benjamin Hardy calls them *default settings*—roles and routines you didn't consciously choose but still play out every day[72]—the fixer, the dependable one, the achiever, the selfless giver, the strong one. These defaults sound noble. They feel familiar, but ask yourself, "Are they true or just very well rehearsed?" Carl Rogers would call these *conditions of worth*—the subconscious belief that love, belonging, or value must be earned by being a certain way, by suppressing the parts of you that didn't fit the script.[73]

This is the foundation of incongruence when the story you're living no longer reflects the person you're becoming, and that's where the Conscious Cut becomes necessary. You cannot move into authorship if you're still living on autopilot. You can't revise your identity while defending roles you never chose. You can't become who you are while protecting the person others needed you to be. The question becomes this: "What parts of my personality were inherited, not chosen? What roles do I keep performing, not because they're aligned but because they're expected?"

If you don't examine your inherited scripts, they'll run your life. If you defend your default settings, you'll remain a character in someone *else's* story while calling that character you. Perhaps Carl Jung said it best when he wrote, "Until you make the unconscious conscious, it will direct your life and you will call it fate." But you're not a role. You're not a label. You're not a static personality built to keep others comfortable.

You're a living, conscious author, and now it's time to choose which parts of the story still belong. That is where the Conscious Cut becomes a scalpel, not a sword. You don't have to destroy everything. You just have to start telling the truth, such as the following:

- I'm still playing the hero because I'm afraid of being seen as weak.
- I always say yes because I was taught that saying no makes you selfish.
- I stay agreeable because I don't know who I'd be without approval.

This isn't weakness; this is awareness. And awareness is what gives you the power to Edit on purpose and intentionally. Pick up the pen, read the lines you've been living, and underline the ones that feel hollow. When the time is right, start cutting because the person you're becoming doesn't need every old role. You don't need to keep pretending that how you've always been is the limit of who you're allowed to become. You're not a fixed script. You're a conscious draft in motion, and the next cut is not a rejection of who you are. It's a reckoning with what no longer fits.

YOUR IDENTITY ISN'T A FACT; IT'S A DRAFT

FROM FIXING TO AUTHORING

At some point, if you're doing the work, you'll hit a wall. You will have read the books, taken the assessments, done the journaling, and named the scripts, the habits, and the patterns. And yet you'll still feel stuck. That's because the old self won't hold anymore, but the new one hasn't taken shape yet. This is the in-between. This is liminality.

The concept of liminality refers to a transitional phase in your life—a phase that involves ambiguity and the dissolution of order that opens a fluid or more malleable space in which new ideas, practices, and identities may emerge and develop. In this liminal space, the temptation is to double down on fixing, to keep treating yourself like a problem to be solved. But you're not a *problem*; you're a *draft*. This next version of you won't emerge from more analysis. It will emerge from authorship. That is the existential pivot.

You're not here to discover who you are. You're here to decide who you're willing to become, not by reaching for another framework, not by achieving some higher level of awareness, but by living into the discomfort of agency. This is the shift that Marcia Baxter Magolda called *self-authorship*—the ability to internally define your beliefs, identity, and direction, not in rebellion, not in reaction, but in rhythm with what you now know is true.[74] Her work showed that self-authorship doesn't arise when we feel clear. It arises when we feel responsible, when we stop looking outside for definitions and start shaping life from the inside out.

Philosophers such as Edmund Husserl knew this long before the language of professional and personal development caught up. Here's what he wrote:

THE RECURRENCE EFFECT

> Prior to all theory the world is given. All opinions, warranted or not, popular, superstitious, and scientific ones—they all refer to the world already given in advance.... No theorizing can contradict this sense.... To seek for more has no meaning.[75]

What he's saying is this: Before you define yourself, explain yourself, or fix yourself, your life is already happening. So before you try to analyze it, justify it, or make a framework for it, you have to live it. Reality doesn't need your permission to exist. It's already here.

The question isn't "What do I believe about myself?" The real question is this: "What has already shown up in my tension, in my patterns, in my quiet moments of doubt or resolve?" You don't need another framework to tell you who you are. You need to return to the givenness of your experience and decide what you're willing to do with it.

That is where the Conscious Cut becomes something more powerful than a mirror. It becomes a compass, not to judge where you are but to reorient toward what matters most. This isn't a stage at which you arrive. There's no final level where you get to say, "I've made it. This is the real me. I'm done." That is just another performance.

The point isn't to become someone. The point is to return again and again to the choices that shape the self you're willing to live. Recent research on self-authorship reinforces that. A 2018 article from the Global Community for Academic Advising highlights how meaningful identity development doesn't emerge from clarity but from provocative moments—those disruptive, tension-filled experiences that force us to reflect, reorient, and rewrite.[76] The process is recursive, not linear.

YOUR IDENTITY ISN'T A FACT; IT'S A DRAFT

Each decision becomes a new chance to shift toward coherence rather than compliance. That's why the Conscious Cut exists—not to mark progress but to offer a rhythm of return, a way back to alignment when drift sets in. What does that look like?

It looks like letting go of the pressure to fix what's not broken. It looks like pausing before you default to old roles. It looks like asking things such as this: "Is this action mine or just familiar? Does this belief serve who I'm becoming or who I was told to be? Is this obligation aligned or inherited?" Then you decide—not once, not perfectly, but courageously—because authorship isn't a one-time act; it's a posture. The Conscious Cut is not your trophy; it's a compass to help you reorient when you drift.

That is the difference between fixing and authoring. Fixing says, "I'm broken; I need to be more." Authoring says, "I'm in motion, and I choose what matters." Fixing seeks validation; authoring seeks coherence. Fixing polishes; authoring cuts. This isn't about improving. It's about returning to what matters, to what aligns with what you're now willing to carry forward, not because it's expected but because it's yours.

REFLECTION PAUSE

The Conscious Cut is a phenomenological act. You're not imposing a theory on your life. You're responding to what's already been given—the feelings, the patterns, the pain, the glimpses of alignment. You're not waiting for someone else to validate your direction. You're describing what you've lived and choosing consciously what comes next.

👁 AWAKEN

- What parts of your life are you still trying to fix instead of author?
- Where have you traded your own lived experience for someone else's definition of growth?

📍 REMEMBER

- You are not a theory waiting to be proven. You're a life already being lived.
- The conscious cut is not a place to reach. It's a tool to return to what's real.

↩ RETURN

- What do you already know—not in your head but in your gut—that needs to be cut?
- What's one small act of authorship you can take today to stop performing and start shaping?

DRIFT HAPPENS WHEN WE CONFUSE FAMILIARITY WITH TRUTH

Let's be honest. Drift doesn't always arrive like an alarm. Sometimes it arrives like comfort—comfort in the routine, comfort in the familiar role, comfort in the safe default. And because it feels good, we assume it's honest. The problem is that anything that feels familiar can start to feel true. Israeli-American psychologist Daniel Kahneman wrote, "A reliable way to make people believe in falsehoods is frequent repetition."[77] That is because familiarity

YOUR IDENTITY ISN'T A FACT; IT'S A DRAFT

is not easily distinguished from truth. Authoritarian institutions and marketers have always known this.

In other words, if something sounds like truth often enough—even when it isn't—your brain might stop questioning it. That's how familiarity becomes identity, not because it's real but because it's repeated. That's why we confuse comfort with coherence. The storyline of who we've always been starts to feel solid, even if the interior has long gone hollow.

Familiarity does not equal truth, but it can trick you into thinking it does. That is where the Conscious Cut becomes essential. It's not just for the big edits, the dramatic turns, or the grand gestures. It's for the micro-adjustments, the ordinary moments where you quietly return to something just because it's easier such as a tone, a script, a belief you've outgrown but haven't examined, or a default identity you never consented to but still carry.

That's the real danger of drift. You don't even notice you're disappearing into it. We cut, not out of violence but out of clarity. We ask, "Am I living this because it's true or because it's familiar?" That question is the invitation back to presence. Maurice Merleau-Ponty said it clearly: "The phenomenological world is not the bringing to explicit expression of a pre-existing being, but the laying down of being. Philosophy is not the reflection of a pre-existing truth, but, like art, the act of bringing truth into being."[78]

Truth isn't behind you. It's not a map someone left for you to find. Truth is something you bring into being through attention, through decision, and through returns. That's what drift erodes—not your morals, not your intelligence, but your orientation to what's real. The Conscious Cut restores what drift erodes.

Here's your invitation. Disrupt the default. Interrupt the rhythm that no longer fits, and cut—not everything, not all at once, just the line that isn't yours anymore because you don't have to burn it down. You just have to stop calling it home.

BEGIN YOUR EDIT WITH A RED PEN

You've made it this far. You've looked at the draft of you, not with shame but with clarity. You've seen the defaults, the roles, and the lines that no longer fit. Now it's time to act, but not by rewriting your entire life. That's a trap. You don't need to reinvent the story. You just need a red pen. Helen Keller said, "I long to accomplish a great and noble task, but it is my chief duty to accomplish small tasks as if they were great and noble. The world is moved along, not only by the mighty shoves of its heroes, but also the aggregate of the tiny pushes of each honest worker."

One Edit, one honest sentence scratched out—that's where becoming begins, where the Conscious Cut becomes real. It's where noticing isn't enough and revision begins. Not everything needs to go. Not everything is broken, but something isn't true anymore, and you already know what it is.

Start with one honest cut. That's how you live into the next draft, not with declarations but with decisions—small, specific, and honest. This isn't about punishing your past; it's about aligning with your future. You're not erasing where you've been. You're releasing what no longer fits. That's the difference between Editing and reacting. Reacting is reckless; Editing is precise. Reacting tries to fix; Editing tries to tell the truth. You don't become someone new by imagining the best version of yourself. You begin by getting honest about what's no longer true. As Carl Jung wrote, "People will do anything, no matter how absurd, in order to avoid facing their own souls."[79]

YOUR IDENTITY ISN'T A FACT; IT'S A DRAFT

You do not become enlightened by imagining figures of light but by making the darkness conscious. That's what the Conscious Cut does. It doesn't promise perfection. It brings the unconscious into view. It asks you to stop pretending, to stop rehearsing, and to face what you've been avoiding. It isn't about becoming enlightened; it's about becoming clear and then doing something about it. So grab the red pen.

Cut the line you're tired of saying. Cut the habit that feels like a costume. Cut the commitment that doesn't carry meaning anymore. Cut the belief that was useful until it became a prison. You don't have to do it all at once. You don't have to explain it to anyone. You just have to name what you've finished rehearsing and then stop rehearsing it. Psychology professor Mihaly Csikszentmihalyi wrote, "Control of consciousness determines the quality of life."[80] Where your attention goes is where your life is written.

You aren't just Editing your story. You're Editing your reality, and every Conscious Cut pulls your attention back from the drift—back to what matters, back to what's real. Editing isn't about who you were. It's about who you're willing to become—in public, in private, and especially when no one's watching.

RETURN FROM THE DRIFT

Every small act of alignment makes the next cut easier because Editing—like becoming—is cumulative. Don't wait for perfect clarity. Don't wait until you feel ready because you never will. Ready doesn't come first. The cut does, and that cut is the first sentence of your next paragraph.

👁 AWAKEN

- Where are you mistaking consistency for truth?
- What part of your identity are you clinging to because it's familiar, not because it fits?

📍 REMEMBER

- Identity isn't something you find. It's something you write again and again.
- You don't need to become someone new. You need to stop performing who you're not.

↩ RETURN

- What belief, role, or assumption could you revise even slightly today?
- What would it look like to live one sentence closer to who you're becoming?

You've picked up the pen. You've made the first cut. You've begun to Edit—not to impress but to align. You've named what's no longer true. You've interrupted the drift. You've reclaimed the right to author this version of yourself. Now comes the part we often ignore—not the writing, not the Editing, but the releasing. Letting go isn't just emotional; it's existential.

You're not just scratching out words on a page. You're cutting versions of yourself that once felt necessary—parts of you that helped you survive, roles that earned you love, and identities that gave you safety. The next step is not theoretical; it's costly.

YOUR IDENTITY ISN'T A FACT; IT'S A DRAFT

You want clarity. You're going to have to give something up. You want alignment. It will ask for a piece of who you used to be. The Edit has been made. Now you have to let go of what *was* so you can carry forward what *is*. That's the threshold we cross next, not into what's easy but into what's true. Letting go will cost you something, and that's how you know it matters.

CHAPTER 11

THE PAIN OF PRECISION

*Man cannot remake himself without suffering,
for he is both the marble and the sculptor.*

ALEXIS CARREL

This is the knife of becoming. We love the idea of change, but when it demands exacting cuts, we hesitate. It's easy to dream about transformation when it's abstract, but when the blade finally touches your life, your habits, or your identity, suddenly every Edit feels like an amputation. That is where most people stop Editing and try to rearrange, polish, or add layers of decoration. They make their lives look differently, but deep down nothing has really changed.

Why are we tempted to avoid Editing? It's because Editing

THE RECURRENCE EFFECT

is painful. It cuts into something you once leaned on, something that gave you an identity, belonging, or safety. Even though you know it doesn't fit anymore, letting it go feels like a betrayal. This is the cut of clarity—the ache of releasing what once worked but no longer serves who you are becoming.

Neuroscience explains why Editing is so hard and feels so painful. Our brains evolved with a built-in loss aversion bias. Research shows that losses are felt at roughly twice the intensity of equivalent gains.[81] If you lose a hundred dollars one day, winning a hundred dollars the next day will not neutralize your pain over the loss. Losses sting far more when it comes to your identity. Letting go of a habit, a role, or a relationship can feel like losing a limb even if that loss cleared space for something truer. Our neural pathways are carved through repetition, and so familiarity—even when it's harmful—feels safe. Leaving an unhealthy rhythm may feel like standing on the edge of a cliff because your nervous system interprets it as danger. Danish philosopher Søren Kierkegaard described this feeling centuries ago when he said, "Anxiety is the dizziness of freedom."[82] That dizziness or vertigo is what you feel when the old scaffolding is gone and nothing familiar is left to hold onto.

It makes sense that we cling to what's familiar, but make no mistake, clinging costs more than cutting. Editing requires precision and practice. That is where Conscious Cut filters act like thresholds. They don't give you easy answers. They reveal what's real.

- **CLARITY > COMFORT:** The first filter often exposes where we've been hiding in familiarity. It asks, "Is this clear or just comfortable? Would I still choose this if I wasn't afraid?" That's a brutal question because clarity rarely feels good in the moment. It unsettles. It destabilizes, but it's also the only way to coherence.

THE PAIN OF PRECISION

- **COST = COMMITMENT:** Every real Edit has a price. If you're not giving something up, you're not really Editing. You're rearranging. This filter asks, "What am I giving up to grow? Where am I faking the cost of becoming?" If you feel no loss, no disruption, or no grief, then your cut hasn't yet reached the bone.

- **WORTH RETURNING TO:** Precision hurts now but builds rhythm later. This filter asks, "Would I be proud to repeat this choice? Is this building a rhythm I respect?" These questions save you from impulse cuts that feel good in the moment but create regret down the line.

- **AGENCY > APPROVAL:** This is where the cut gets personal. When you start choosing for yourself instead of performing for others, you will disappoint someone, and that's the point. The filter asks, "Am I editing to reflect what I know is true or to maintain how I'm seen?" Edits made for applause will always come undone, but the ones made in solitude with no guarantee of validation are the ones that mark the shift from performance to authorship.

- **ALIGNMENT > ACHIEVEMENT:** This filter cuts through the noise of metrics and milestones. It asks, "Does this choice move me toward the person I said I wanted to become or just make me look successful?" Achievement without alignment feels hollow, like winning someone else's game. This cut demands internal coherence, not external comparison. You may lose status, recognition, or comfort, but you gain the kind of peace that doesn't need to be seen to be real.

THE RECURRENCE EFFECT

These filters force you to pay attention to the real intention of transformation.

Pain is proof. The pain you feel in precision is not evidence that you're failing; it's evidence that you're touching something real. As existential psychologist Kirk Schneider writes, "Our greatest challenge today . . . is to couple conviction with doubt."[83] In this context, conviction means pragmatically developed faith, trust, or centeredness. Doubt means openness to the ongoing changeability, mystery, and fallibility of the conviction.

This paradox is the core of every real cut. Conviction without doubt becomes arrogance or rigidity. Doubt without conviction dissolves into drift. Precision forces you to hold both at once. You cut because you are convicted that something no longer belongs. Yet you step into the mystery of what comes next without guarantees, and yes, it hurts. It's supposed to because every real cut tears an illusion and demands both courage and humility.

Pain in this context is not punishment; it's proof. It's proof that you've moved past performance, proof that you're authoring a new draft. Think of it this way. If the cut doesn't hurt at least a little, it probably wasn't deep enough to matter.

Most people underestimate the grief they feel in the Editing process. Cuts don't just cost us habits. They cost us versions of ourselves. Precision feels like grief because it *is* grief. You're laying to rest an old identity—one that once protected you. You don't erase it, and you don't dishonor it, but you do release it.

Grief is always the companion of release. Psychologists note that even positive transitions—new jobs, healthier rhythms, leaving toxic relationships—carry grief because they require identity death.[84] We mourn what we let go of even when we don't want it back. This grief is not a sign you've made the wrong cut. It's a sign that the cut is real.

THE PAIN OF PRECISION

We need trusted people to witness our cuts. When you're in the ache of precision, you will second-guess yourself. You'll bargain. You'll tell yourself you can carry the weight just a little bit longer. A true witness won't let you slide back into illusion. They won't rescue you or soften the edge. They'll stand with you in the silence of the cut and remind you that this pain is not proof of failure. It's proof of becoming. Without witnesses you will almost always retreat to safety. With them you can stay long enough in the ache for the cut to take root.

Every cut is a paradox. You cut because you're convicted that something no longer belongs, but you step forward in doubt, open to what might emerge. Conviction stabilizes you. Doubt keeps you honest. That tension is a threshold of transformation.

Edits aren't only about what you release; they're also about what remains. Every no is a yes to something else. Every word you strike from the draft gives more weight to the ones that stay. That's the hidden cost of clarity. It reveals what you've truly chosen to keep. What you keep is who you'll become.

WHAT YOU KEEP IS WHO YOU'LL BECOME

Letting go hurts, but the greater challenge is realizing that your becoming is shaped not by what you cut away but by what you choose to carry forward. Every decision is double-edged—to release one thing is to reinforce another. That is why precision is more than subtraction; it's authorship. You are declaring what stays in the story, and the lines you refuse to strike become the spine of your next draft. Think of it this way. Your identity is not only carved by what you lose but by what you preserve. Every preserved pattern, habit, or conviction will echo into the future version of yourself.

THE RECURRENCE EFFECT

Most of us fool ourselves into thinking that keeping is neutral, that it's safer to hold on than to let go. But that's a lie. Keeping always carries a cost. Keeping the wrong thing consumes time, attention, and energy that could be invested elsewhere. Neuroscience will actually back this up. Cognitive load theory shows that the brain's working memory is limited.[85] Every role, belief, or habit that you *keep* takes up mental bandwidth. Holding on to too much chokes your capacity to focus on what actually matters. The question isn't whether keeping has a cost. The question is whether the cost is worth it.

That is why the pain of precision isn't just about loss; it's about authorship. You are not just crossing things out. You're selecting what gets to define your next version. Think of a sculptor carving a block of stone. The marble removed is significant, but what remains is the sculpture. The cut only matters because of what's left. Your becoming works the same way. The Edits of your life, both cuts and keeps, are chiseling the figure you're becoming out of the block of time you've been given.

The somewhat brutal truth hidden in this metaphor is that you're both the sculptor and the marble. French surgeon and biologist Alexis Carrel wrote, "Man cannot remake himself without suffering, for he is both the marble and the sculptor." That's why it hurts. Every edit cuts into your own flesh. Every strike of the chisel reshapes *you*, not something external to yourself. You are shaping *yourself* while feeling the blows.

Neuroscience shows that when you release an old belief, role, or rhythm, your brain experiences prediction error—the jolt of realizing that the pattern and expectations no longer apply. That triggers a stress response because the brain is designed to conserve energy by relying on familiar pathways. Breaking those pathways feels threatening at a primal level.[86]

THE PAIN OF PRECISION

But here's the paradox: That suffering is also the raw material of growth. Every time you let go, your brain experiences neuroplasticity—the process of rewiring itself to form new connections, new habits, and new perspectives. New rhythms only emerge when the old circuits are pruned. In other words, the cut and the keep are both biological. You literally feel the chisel strike because your nervous system is being reshaped in real time.

That means becoming isn't a smooth ascent; it's jagged. It hurts because the brain doesn't quietly update itself. It resists, it protests, and it grieves, and yet that very resistance signals that you're in the territory of evolution. The temptation, of course, is to stop striking, to leave the block intact, to convince yourself that "whole" means "uncut"—but that's an illusion.

Refusing to sculpt doesn't preserve your life; it fossilizes it. Precision even when it wounds is the only path to coherence. The question is never whether becoming will hurt. The question is whether you're willing to suffer the blows of authorship, knowing that every strike is creating a form you can live inside.

That is why witnesses matter just as much here as they did in the letting go. It's because we are notoriously blind to the weight of what we keep. A witness can help you see whether your "yes" is coherence or convenience—whether what you've chosen to carry forward is really yours or just familiar baggage and disguise. Witnessing doesn't mean judgment. It means having someone to ask, "Is this worth returning to?" If it's not, then keeping it is just another way of drifting.

To keep is to commit. To keep is to declare, "This will shape me." That's why what you keep is not just preference; it's responsibility. You are responsible for the rhythms you preserve, for the patterns you rehearse, and for the relationships you protect because they will shape not just who you *are* but who you're *becoming*.

THE RECURRENCE EFFECT

If you want to become someone worth returning to, you cannot afford to keep carelessly. Of course, not everything you keep is only about you. Old versions of yourself don't die quietly. The ghosts of past identities linger in the expectations of others and the roles they still want you to play. The moment you let go of one version, someone else may cling to it for you. That means the work of Editing is never purely personal. It's relational, and that's where the real haunting begins.

THE GHOST OF OLD IDENTITIES

Every version of you that once lived still echoes in the minds of others. Friends, family, and colleagues remember you as you were, and they expect you to keep playing that role. You may cut a line from your draft, but someone else is still reading it aloud. When you refuse to keep performing it, they feel abandoned, betrayed, or even threatened because your shift doesn't just unsettle you, it unsettles your entire ecosystem. That is the truth we often forget.

Editing your life isn't a solitary act. It's relational, and ghosts of old identities will come knocking, asking you to put the mask back on. There's a biological reason for this resistance. Human beings are prediction machines. Just as your own brain builds pathways of expectations, so do the people around you over time. They come to rely on your patterns, your behaviors, your reactions, and your roles as anchors of stability. These expectations aren't just mental shortcuts. They're embedded in the body through neural wiring.[87]

Every time you show up in a certain way, your brain forms associated links: *This is who she is. This is how he responds. This is how I can predict them.* Those pathways get reinforced through mirror neurons, the brain's relational circuitry that allows us to

THE PAIN OF PRECISION

synchronize with one another. It's why the mood spreads in a room, why laughter catches on, and why one person's anxiety can raise the tension of a whole team.

Mirror neurons create resonance. They allow people to *feel* you in ways that bypass conscious thought. When you break a pattern, you're not just rewiring your *own* brain; you're disrupting *theirs*. You're creating what neuroscientists call prediction error—that uncomfortable jolt of the brain when it realizes the world doesn't match its expectation. It's the same circuitry that makes you jump when a friend suddenly swerves while driving or when an unexpected note in a familiar song feels jarring. The brain dislikes broken patterns because they create uncertainty, and uncertainty feels like danger.

When you start showing up differently, when you say no instead of yes, when you stop performing, or when you drop an old role, you trigger prediction errors in the people around you. They don't just notice it; they *feel* it in their nervous system, and most people don't like that. That's why they resist, not always out of malice but out of their own longing for stability. Their biology wants the world to stay predictable, and if their world includes you, then they want you to stay predictable. They may nudge, pressure, guilt, or shame you back into the familiar groove, not because they consciously want to hold you back but because your change threatens the coherence of their map of reality.

Here's the deeper challenge. Resistance isn't just external. It can become internalized. Since we are social creatures, our nervous systems are deeply attuned to approval and belonging. When others push back against your evolution, your body interprets it as risk—sometimes even as a survival threat. The amygdala fires, cortisol spikes, and suddenly growth feels unsafe. The pain of Editing isn't only the loss of what you release; it's also the stress of others pushing against your new coherence. That is why preparation matters.

You must expect resistance. You must normalize it and even welcome it as a sign you are actually evolving. If no one is unsettled—including you—then the cut probably wasn't deep enough. That is why witnesses matter even more. When the old community clings to the old you, you need a new one to hold the line, people who won't collapse you back into their comfort but can stand in the discomfort with you. You need witnesses who know the biology of resistance and can remind you that *their* prediction error is not *your* failure. Their unease is not your call to return. Stay with the cut because the truth is that you cannot evolve without disturbing someone else's map of you, and you cannot carry their maps in your own becoming at the same time. One will always collapse into the other.

Simone de Beauvoir understood that tension when she said, "I tore myself away from the safe comfort of certainties through my love for truth, and the truth rewarded me."[88] The ghosts of old identities embody those certainties—those roles, habits, and performances that once gave coherence. Even if they are false, releasing them means not only grieving but also risking the grief of others. Their loss is not of *you* but of the *version of you* that propped up their story.

That's why Editing feels lonely. In the silence after the cut, you lose not only illusion but also applause. We like to imagine identity as an individual, but it is also ecological. Who you are is coauthored in the space between you and others. That means every cut reverberates through your relationships. Your choice to cut may destabilize an entire network—family dynamics, workplace cultures, and communities that rely on the old you.

This is where Agency > Approval becomes more than a filter. It

THE PAIN OF PRECISION

becomes survival. If you cut only what others will tolerate, you're not authoring; you're appeasing. The cost of keeping approval will be the death of coherence. But here's the paradox. While your cuts may disrupt others, they also invite them. Your release can serve as a witness for their own. Your courage to face the ghost of an old identity may free them to face their own.

Neuroscience adds another level here. Psychologist Donald Hebb said, "Neurons that fire together wire together."[89] That is the principle that repeated patterns of thoughts, feelings, and behaviors strengthen the neural circuits that carry them. Over time, those pathways become like grooves in the brain, well-worn tracks that the nervous system defaults to without effort or thought. But here's the part we often miss. In the same way that Editing is personal and resistance to your Edits is external, these grooves are equally relational.

Patterns of self are reinforced not only inside your brain but in the brains of those around you. Every time you perform a role and someone responds to it, that loop wires deeper. Every time someone laughs at your joke, praises your performance, or expects you to react a certain way, it cements the circuit. That is why ghosts of old identities feel so heavy. They aren't just memories you carry. They're embodied, rehearsed neural networks living simultaneously in your nervous system and in the nervous systems of everyone you've touched.

You may want to let go of an old identity, but every person who still treats you like the old you is firing that circuitry again. Because mirror neurons allow us to sync with others, their expectations can reignite the very patterns you're trying to release in order to let go of an old identity. You're not just pushing against your own wiring; you're pushing against the wiring of an entire relational ecosystem.

THE RECURRENCE EFFECT

It feels like a battle because biologically it is. You're not fighting one ghost but dozens, maybe hundreds, depending on how long that role has lived in the world. Every family member, every colleague, and every friend who has rehearsed that version of you carries a shard of its circuitry. When you change, you don't just grieve it alone. Others feel its absence, too, and often resist.

That is why change can feel so lonely. You're not just grieving your own ghost; you're standing against the collective reinforcement of everyone else's ghosts of you. That weight is real, and your nervous system feels that every time someone pulls you back into an old rhythm. Ghosts don't vanish because you've decided to cut them. They linger in the circuitry of relationships, showing up at family gatherings, workplace meetings, and even in your own body. When you walk into spaces tied to the old identity, they live in the environment, which means part of Editing is environmental—choosing where you return, who you return to, and what echoes you allow to keep sounding.

That is why witnessing matters so profoundly. Without witnesses who can see you beyond your ghosts, you will always be tempted to collapse back into them. A true witness doesn't help you cut. They help you resist resurrection. They stand with you when the battle is not against your own willpower but against the weight of collective neural rehearsal. So yes, it feels like a battle because on a neurological and relational level, it is. If you're not prepared for that, the ghost will win.

That is why community matters—not the community that clings to your ghost but the one willing to hold space for your Edits. You need witnesses who will not collapse you back into the safety of old roles but witnesses who can bear to see you stumble in your becoming without trying to resurrect the version of you that made them comfortable. To cut alone is almost impossible.

THE PAIN OF PRECISION

Yes, the act of authorship is profoundly personal. Only you can choose the cut. Only you can decide what stays and what goes. But sustaining that choice in the long shadow of resistance, both your own and others, requires support.

Neuroscience helps explain why human nervous systems are built for coregulation from birth. Our survival depends on it. A child's stress response calms only when it's met with the attuned presence of a caregiver.[90] That wiring never goes away. Even as adults, our capacity to hold tension, tolerate uncertainty, and endure the anxiety of becoming expands in the presence of others who can stay steady with us. A calm witness doesn't erase your ghosts, but their presence helps you hold the line against them.

That's why witnessing is not optional. It's essential. Without it, the biology of becoming will betray you. The social pull of approval will drag you back to the performance. The ghost will whisper louder, promising relief if you just put the mask back on. In your exhaustion, you'll be tempted, not because you're weak but because you're human. A true witness interrupts that collapse. They hold the mirror when you can't. They remind you that your grief is proof of the cut, not a reason to undo it. They let the old version die without resurrecting it, and they grieve it with you— not for the illusion but for the courage it takes to release it.

That is also why discernment matters. Not every community can hold your cuts. Some are too invested in the roles you've always played. They'll keep summoning your ghosts, not because they hate you but because they *need* you to stay predictable. Witnesses—the right ones—choose coherence over their own comfort. They won't let nostalgia or convenience outweigh your authorship.

Here's the paradox: The work of Editing is yours alone, but it can almost never be done alone. Your hand holds the knife, but it's the presence of witnesses that steadies it. When you falter without them, you trade authorship for appeasement, you go back to performing, and the ghost wins. Letting go will not only cost you something; it will cost others something—and not everyone is willing to pay that price with you. Some will cling. Some will leave. Some will resent. But coherence cannot be built on performance.

RETURN FROM THE DRIFT

The price of authorship is relational disruption. The reward is a rhythm that belongs to you and eventually, perhaps, a community of witnesses who chooses to meet you there. That leads to the next threshold. The question is not just "What will you cut?" but "Why are you cutting?" and "Are you Editing for comfort or for truth?"

AWAKEN

- What parts of your life are you trying to Edit out, not because they're wrong but because they no longer fit the story you were told to live?
- Where have you confused self-awareness with self-authorship?

REMEMBER

- The Conscious Cut is not a goal to reach; it's a guide to return.
- You are not a concept. You are a conscious draft in motion.

THE PAIN OF PRECISION

> ← **RETURN**

- What tension in your life is asking to be named instead of analyzed?
- What decision could shift you from performance to authorship?

ARE YOU EDITING FOR COMFORT OR FOR TRUTH?

Not all cuts are equal. Some pruning is performance. Some is liberation. We love the drama of Editing—the ritual of the big announcement, the bold claim, the grand gesture that says, "See, I'm changing." But not all cuts go deep enough. Some are made to look courageous when in reality they leave the heart of the old pattern untouched. That's performance Editing. It feels good at the moment because it earns applause. But applause is not the same as authorship.

Liberation Editing, by contrast, rarely looks dramatic. It's quieter. It doesn't always post well on social media. Sometimes it looks like saying no in private, refusing to explain yourself, or grieving silently as you let go of something familiar. Liberation doesn't always come with recognition; it comes with coherence.

The danger is falling into the comfort trap. Many people cut for comfort, not for truth. They cut what feels easy to cut, what won't disturb too much, and what won't cost them the approval of others. These cuts give the illusion of movement but keep them exactly where they are. Again, neuroscience indicates why this happens. When the brain anticipates loss, it triggers a stress response. Cortisol rises, the amygdala lights up, and the body screams, "Don't do this!" Your entire nervous system interprets letting go as danger because it evolved to equate the unfamiliar with threat.[91]

In that moment, comfort Editing offers relief. You can make a small cosmetic cut and feel instantly better. The brain rewards you with a bit of dopamine for doing something new, even if it changes nothing at the core. You get the satisfaction of novelty without the grief of real loss. But the relief is temporary. The deeper misalignment remains, and eventually the fracture reappears.

Cutting for truth, on the other hand, forces you into discomfort. It doesn't soothe; it unsettles. It activates the body's alarm systems because you're not only breaking your own neural patterns but also disrupting the relational expectations of others. You're creating prediction errors everywhere—in your mind, in your body, and in your community. That is why it feels destabilizing. It's not proof that you're failing. It's proof that the cut is real. If it shakes you, it's because you struck bone. If it hurts, it's because the knife has finally reached something that mattered.

You have to be willing to sit with the discomfort. Discomfort is not the obstacle; it's the only way through. If you rush to escape it, you short-circuit the process. You return to performance, to comfort, to drift. But if you can stay with it, if you can breathe through the alarm bells long enough, something new begins to emerge. That is the miracle of neuroplasticity, the rewiring of your brain as old patterns weaken and new ones take hold. That rewiring requires tension, stress, and even grief—no discomfort, no existential evolution.

This is the work of authorship, what Kierkegaard called "the dizziness of freedom." Kirk Schneider calls it "the coupling of conviction with doubt." Sitting in discomfort is the proof that you are alive in your freedom, not numbing yourself with illusions of safety. As you move forward, know this: What is coming

THE PAIN OF PRECISION

will not feel easy. It will not feel smooth. You'll want to retreat to comfort. But if you do, you'll never know the marrow-deep coherence that comes from truth. Discomfort is not the enemy; it's the evidence. It's the doorway. Your capacity to sit with it will determine whether the cut becomes liberation or just another performance. So take this seriously. The next pages are not about theory. They're about practice—practice that will demand that you stand in the fire of discomfort long enough for the cut to take root.

This is not punishment; it is proof—proof that you are no longer performing, proof that you are becoming. If you can sit with the discomfort, you'll walk through. If you cannot, you'll retreat. The choice between those two is the choice of your life.

The Conscious Cut filters can protect you from self-deception.

- **CLARITY > COMFORT:** Ask yourself, "Is this cut giving me relief, or is it giving me coherence for a version of me worth returning to? Would I make this Edit again tomorrow?" A true cut isn't just a release; it's a rhythm.

- **WORTH RETURNING TO:** If you wouldn't be proud to repeat it, you're not cutting for coherence. You're chasing a moment, and moments don't build momentum. Rhythm does.

- **COST = COMMITMENT:** Real Editing costs something—time, identity, and belonging. If you feel no loss, you haven't touched the truth.

- **AGENCY > APPROVAL:** Ask yourself, "Who is this Edit for?" If the answer is the crowd, it's a performance. If the answer is coherence, even without applause, it's liberation.

- **ALIGNMENT > ACHIEVEMENT:** If it earns approval but betrays your becoming, it's not liberation; it's sedation. The deeper cut always sacrifices the optics of progress for the integrity of evolution. Choose alignment, even if it means letting go of a win that was never really yours.

To cut for truth is to disappoint someone, sometimes even yourself. It's to face the gap between who you've been and who you're becoming without dressing it up for comfort. It's to accept that liberation will sometimes look like failure from the outside. The truth always outlasts comfort. Comfort cuts may preserve peace in the moment, but they create fractures later. Liberation cuts may rupture now, but they create coherence that holds.

Again, the witness is crucial here because when you're standing at the threshold between comfort and truth, you will rationalize. You'll tell yourself the easy cut was enough. A true witness refuses to collude with your performance. They'll ask the harder question: "Did this cut actually free you, or did it just make you look free?" Without those voices, you'll always drift toward comfort. With them, you're held accountable to the truth.

THE RELEASE RITUAL

American poet Charles Bukowski wrote, "What matters most is how well you walk through the fire."[92] Release is fire. It's not neat, painless, or safe. It burns because you're laying to rest a version of yourself that once held you together. The temptation, even here, will be to romanticize the letting go—to make it tidy, to script it like closure. But this isn't closure; it's combustion. The ritual of release is not about erasing your past. It's about refusing to keep

THE PAIN OF PRECISION

carrying it. It is about walking through fire without turning back, without numbing the heat, and without pretending it doesn't hurt. The measure of this fire isn't how cleanly you get through it but whether you keep walking.

Discomfort doesn't mean you failed the ritual. It means you're in it. The grief, the ache, the raw absence you feel after the cut—that is the proof you've touched what's real. Ritual is the fire made visible. It takes what has been smoldering in your mind and puts it into your body. Without ritual, Edits remain abstract. With ritual, they become thresholds you can feel in your bones. Ritual is how you declare to yourself—and to whatever witnesses you invite—that the cut is not just an idea. It's real, it's final, it hurts, and it matters.

While walking through fire, the ritual does not need to be elaborate. It needs to be honest. Here's one way to walk through it.

- **NAME IT:** Write down the story, the role, and the identity you're releasing. Be ruthless. Precision burns. Don't soften the language. Write the sentence that sears.

- **WITNESS IT:** Read it aloud. Say it to yourself, to a trusted witness, or into the silence of the room. Speaking it aloud fans the flames that deny your safety or makes you pretend it was never real.

- **EULOGIZE IT:** Write a brief eulogy for the version of yourself that you're releasing. Thank it for what it gave you. Name how it once held you, even as you admit why it cannot come with you. Fire doesn't just destroy; it purifies. Grief is the smoke that proves something was consumed.

- **BURN IT:** Destroy the paper, shred it, bury it. Literally set it on fire. Watch it disappear. This is the part that hurts most because disruption makes the loss undeniable.

THE RECURRENCE EFFECT

- **RETURN:** In the ashes, speak one sentence aloud about what you're keeping or who you are becoming. This is a triumph. It's survival. It's coherence, rising from what you chose to burn.

Neuroscience tells us why the fire works. Embodied acts such as writing, speaking, and destroying activate multiple brain systems at once.[93] They encode the memory deeper than thought alone. When you enact release through ritual, you're not just symbolizing the cut, you're rewiring the circuitry tied to the old identity and firing the first sparks of the new. But the truth isn't just biological; it's existential.

Nietzsche warned, "You must be ready to burn yourself in your own flame; how could you rise anew if you have not first become ashes?"[94] This is the real logic of release. You can't bypass the burning. You can't rise while clinging to what was. The old identity has to be reduced to ashes. Only then can something coherent rise in its place. To pretend otherwise is to rehearse, not release.

Phenomenology helps us see why this matters. Life is not lived in abstractions. It's lived in the body, in time, and in relationship, which means release is not a tidy thought experiment. It is a felt event. It shows up in your breath, the tremor in your chest, and the grief that weighs on your shoulders. Becoming is embodied, and embodiment does not lie. You can think you've moved on, but your body knows if you're still carrying the weight.

You never burn alone. Phenomenology reminds us that we are always "being-with." According to Heidegger, this is *Mitsein*.[95] Our identities are coauthored in the presence of others, which means our cuts are too. When witnesses join you, the fire deepens. Their presence literally alters the experience, causing coregulation—two nervous systems, resonating, stabilizing, carrying what

THE PAIN OF PRECISION

one could not carry alone. A true witness doesn't extinguish the flames or rescue you from them. They don't minimize the cost or pull you back into performance. They stand beside you, steady you while you burn, refuse to collapse you back into what's familiar, and don't let you carry the fire in isolation.

In phenomenological terms, their presence constitutes the moment with you. They help make it real. Without them, the temptation to retreat is overwhelming. But with them, you can remain long enough in the fire for the burning to do its work, for the old self to become ashes, and for the coherence to rise from what you've released.

After the ritual, there will be silence—a hollow where the old identity once stood. Your body will ache to fill it, to resurrect what you destroy, to step back into the comfort of familiarity. But absence is not failure; it's space. Fire clears the field so something new can grow. That emptiness is not the end of the ritual. It's the beginning of coherence.

RETURN FROM THE DRIFT

Release doesn't erase the past. It makes room for a future unburdened by what no longer belongs. The fire doesn't leave you the same. It leaves you forged.

◉ AWAKEN

- What version of yourself are you trying to keep alive even though it's expired?
- Where are you resisting grief because you haven't named the loss?

📍 REMEMBER

- You can't align with your future while clinging to your past.
- Shedding isn't failure; it's the final stage of authorship.

↩ RETURN

- What are you willing to lay down so something new can begin?
- What must never return with you, no matter how familiar it feels?

You've cut. You've chosen. You've let go. You've walked through the fire. Now you stand in the silence of the ashes. Nietzsche was right that to rise anew you must first become ashes. That's the cost of coherence. But the question is not whether you can burn once. It's whether you can live in rhythm with the fire. Becoming is not achieved in a single act of release. It's sustained in the practice of return—not the performance, not for applause, but because coherence demands it. The next chapter isn't about ashes. It's about what rises from them and whether you choose to become someone worth returning to.

CHAPTER 12

BECOME SOMEONE WORTH RETURNING TO

To be yourself in a world that is constantly trying to make you something else is the greatest accomplishment.

RALPH WALDO EMERSON

The fire's over. The burning has done its work. What remains are ashes, silence, and absence—the raw space we left behind. The temptation here is to mistake this silence for arrival—to believe the Edit is finished because the ritual is complete. But becoming doesn't end in ashes. It actually begins there.

Return is the practice. It's not a fallback; it's a foundation. Why does return matter? Well, perfection is a myth, and reinvention is an illusion. You don't become someone new once and for all. You

THE RECURRENCE EFFECT

become through repetition, through the daily recommitment to what you've chosen, through the rhythm of returning to coherence, especially when no one's watching. That is the difference between a cut that stays and a cut that becomes flesh. Without return, your release is just a dramatic gesture. With return, it becomes the spine of a new rhythm—a coherence that holds.

Phenomenology reminds us that life is not lived in the abstract. It is lived in the everyday acts of embodiment. You don't experience yourself as an idea. You experience yourself in motion—walking into the room, responding to a voice, holding a silence. Return is the phenomenological ground of becoming. It's the lived repetition where thought and action fuse. Each time you align a choice, a word, or a gesture with the cut you've made, you are inscribing coherence into the fabric of your existence.

Maurice Merleau-Ponty taught that the body is not just an object in the world but the very subject through which we encounter the world.[96] Return, then, is not intellectual rehearsal. It's a bodily act. You practice becoming with your posture, your breath, and your presence. It's how you show up on Monday morning in the small acts you think no one notices.

For Merleau-Ponty, perception is never a detached observation. It's an embodied participation. The body is not a container you live inside. It is the way the world discloses itself to you—the medium through which meaning arrives. Your hand does not simply touch the world. It also feels itself blurring the line between subject and object. In the same way, every act of return is not only something you do in the world; it is how the world comes alive for you again. Because perception is always situated, return is never private. Even the smallest gesture—a nod, a pause, the way you hold silence—carries meaning that others absorb, sometimes without words.

BECOME SOMEONE WORTH RETURNING TO

Merleau-Ponty would say these unnoticed acts are not marginal. They are the very fabric of your becoming, woven into the shared field of existence where self and world continually shape one another.[97] That is why return is not repetition. This is crucial to understand. Return is not repeating. Repetition implies sameness—a mechanical loop where nothing changes—but you are not the same each time you return. The self you bring back has been altered by every decision, every release, and every horizon you've crossed.

Perception is never identical. The world discloses itself differently with each encounter because you are different each time you arrive. Returning, then, is not circling back to the exact same place. It is spiraling deeper into coherence. That distinction matters. Without it, return can sound like stagnation, as if you were trapped in a cycle.

A true return is evolution and rhythm. The practice is constant, but the perspective is new. The rhythm holds, but the song changes. Repetition without change is *drift*. Return with change is *authorship*. The rhythm of return is an expansion on Heidegger's idea of dwelling.[98] Return is not glamorous. It doesn't come with applause. In fact, it often feels ordinary and even dull. But that ordinariness is the point. Grand gestures fade.

The real test of coherence is whether it can withstand the monotony of repetition. That is why phenomenology insists on the everyday as a site of meaning. Martin Heidegger called this dwelling, not simply inhabiting a shelter but being attuned to the world through care, rootedness, and presence. To dwell is to live in rhythm with the earth, the sky, the others we share life with, and the divinities—what he called "the fourfold." In this frame, return is not just habit; it's the way we build our being.

Heidegger argued that to dwell is to live in harmony with four inseparable dimensions of existence.

THE RECURRENCE EFFECT

- **EARTH:** The ground that sustains us—not just the soil but the material and body conditions of life. It's what nourishes and limits us. In return, we're called to care for it, not exploit it.

- **SKY:** The horizon of time and possibility—the cycles of day and night, the seasons. It's the expanse that reminds us of transcendence and infinitude. To return is to notice these rhythms and align with them rather than living as if we were outside of them.

- **DIVINITIES:** Not necessarily gods but the dimension of mystery, reverence, and what lies beyond human control. It is the call to humility and awe, the acknowledgement that not everything can be mastered or explained.

- **MORTALS:** All of us and our finitude. To dwell authentically is to live with the awareness that we are mortal beings, that our time is limited, and therefore our choices matter.

The fourfold isn't a checklist but an interplay. Heidegger said that dwelling happens when we save the earth, receive the sky, await the divinities, and initiate mortals—in other words, care for the world, attune to time, honor mystery, and walk with others in shared mortality.

When we link Heidegger's ideas to the rhythm of return, we see returning as dwelling in the fourfold. Each act of return is earthly. It's embodied, material, and grounded in breath, gesture, or place. Each return is also under the sky—part of the unfolding of days, seasons, and cycles that remind us we're always evolving. Each return acknowledges divinity. Coherence isn't entirely our creation but something we participate in with reverence and care.

BECOME SOMEONE WORTH RETURNING TO

Each return honors our mortality, reminding us that our time is limited and so we must live in fidelity now, not later.

The rhythm of return becomes more than self-discipline. It becomes dwelling—a way of inhabiting the world in coherence with earth, sky, divinities, and mortals. When you return, you are not merely repeating an act. You are reinhabiting a world that has suddenly shifted, and in doing so, you're shaping its architecture. Dwelling for Heidegger is never passive. It's an ongoing responsibility to take care, to preserve, and to let things be what they are—and in letting things be to create a home for your becoming.

The rhythm of return is not a closed loop. It is a way of dwelling where fidelity is measured, not in one-time declarations but in the way you continually inhabit coherence. Each unnoticed act and each return to what matters is a stone in the architecture of your life. You're always building and always dwelling.

To return is also to resist. Every day, ghosts will tug at you. Every day, comfort will whisper. Every day, your body will crave the familiar over the coherent. Return is how you resist drift, not through dramatic declarations but through steady acts of recommitment. That is what it means to live your Edit—your cut—not just declare it. When you return, you prove that coherence is not a performance but a practice.

Here's the question ahead. The tension of this chapter is simple. Will you live your Edit even when no one's watching? Will you keep returning, not for validation but for coherence? Coherence isn't earned in a single release. It's forged in rhythm. You're not becoming through reinvention; you're becoming through return.

THE RECURRENCE EFFECT

THE SMALL ACTS THAT SHAPE US

The problem is that our world has trained us to look for transformation and spectacle. We live in a culture that tells us transformation must be performed, broadcast, and made extraordinary. Novelty gets the clicks. Reinvention gets the applause. We are taught that if it isn't amazing enough to share, it isn't real. But existentially, that is the lie that keeps us lost. Kierkegaard warned of the despair of living outwardly, defining ourselves by reflection in the crowd.[99]

Phenomenology reminds us that meaning isn't in the show. It's in the lived experience, in the way our bodies and choices inscribe coherence in the world moment by moment. You can post endlessly about becoming, but if your body doesn't live it, the coherence isn't real. Musician Nick Cave said the following:

> The everyday human gesture is always a heartbeat away from the miraculous. . . . Ultimately we make things happen through our actions, way beyond our understanding or intention; . . . our seemingly small ordinary human acts have untold consequences; . . . what we do in this world means something; . . . *we are not nothing*; and . . . our most quotidian human actions *by their nature* burst the seams of our intent and spill meaningfully and radically through time and space, changing *everything*. . . . our deeds, no matter how insignificant they may feel, are replete with meaning, and of vast consequence, and . . . they constantly impact upon the unfolding story of the world, whether we know it or not.[100]

This is the truth of grounded becoming. Your smallest, most ordinary acts are not small at all. They ripple outward far beyond what you intend to realize. A single act of coherence—telling the truth when silence would be easier, choosing presence over distraction—can spill meaningfully through time and space, altering not only your story but the story of those closest to you.

Grounded becoming isn't dull; it's alive, embodied, and steady. Remember that Heidegger called this *dwelling*—where we inhabit the world with care through repeated acts that accumulate in a way of being. Grand gestures may inspire you for a moment, but it's a grounded rhythm of return that reshapes you over time.

Ordinary doesn't mean meaningless. Ordinary means embodied. Ordinary means every breath, every pause, and every unnoticed act that can be a sight of coherence. That's what makes it miraculous. It doesn't need to be grand to matter.

RETURN FROM THE DRIFT

The question here is not whether you can reinvent yourself dramatically. The question is whether you can return quietly. Can you inhabit coherence in the ordinary rhythm of your life—not for the spectacle, not for the applause, but for the simple radical act of becoming? In a world addicted to novelty and spectacle, the courage to return quietly is itself a revolutionary act.

👁 AWAKEN

- o Where are you still chasing spectacle instead of trusting the power of the ordinary?
- o What rhythm of return are you resisting because it feels too quiet to prove or remember?

📍 REMEMBER

- Becoming doesn't happen through reinvention; it unfolds through return.
- Integrity isn't perfection; it's fidelity to who you are now and who you are becoming.

↩ RETURN

- What would it look like to practice one small act of coherence today—not for applause but for alignment?
- How can you give your future self something sturdy to stand on by the choice you make right now?

THE INTEGRITY LOOP

If return is the rhythm, then integrity is the loop it creates. Integrity is not a title you claim once. It is the ongoing alignment between what you say and what you do, and between who you claim to be and how you actually live. Like everything else in this world, integrity isn't grand. It's grounded. It's forged in the ordinary rhythm of return—a rhythm that looks quiet to others but costs everything for you.

We tend to imagine integrity as reputation—a static label, something earned once and carried forever. But phenomenology reminds us that integrity is lived, not possessed. It's not an abstract concept but rather the moment-by-moment bodily convergence of word and deed. Each time you keep a promise, even a small one, you close the loop. Each time you betray yourself by saying one thing and doing another, by appeasing for approval instead of acting from coherence, you fracture the loop.

Integrity is experienced, not in theory but in the lived rhythm of your actions. Integrity is not about never failing. It's about noticing the fracture and returning to coherence again and again. This is no casual matter. Integrity is costly. Nietzsche named its severity.

> At every step one has to wrestle for truth; one has had to surrender for it almost everything to which the heart, to which our love, our trust in life, cling otherwise. That requires greatness of soul: the service of truth is the hardest service. What does it mean, after all, to have integrity in matters of the spirit? That one is severe against one's heart, that one despises "beautiful sentiments', that one makes of every Yes and No a matter of conscience.[101]

This is the heart of the integrity loop. Every yes and every no is a matter of conscience—not convenience, not performance, but truth. Integrity demands that you be severe against your heart when your heart wants comfort, nostalgia, or the familiar. That is why integrity loops feel heavy. Each act of alignment—even the smallest—is a struggle, a surrender, and a cost. And yet integrity is not static.

Each loop you close is different because each return brings a different self. You'll never walk into the same moment twice. You never say the same yes twice. You never live the same silence twice. That is what makes the integrity loop more than repetition. It's a spiral, not a circle. Each return deepens coherence, layering your becoming through ordinary but costly acts. Repetition without change is drift. Return with alignment is integrity. But as you noticed and phenomenology insists, lived experience is the ground of meaning.

Integrity isn't measured by what others believe about you. It's measured by the fidelity between your word and your deed lived in the obscurity of the everyday until it shapes you into someone worth returning to. Sartre's warning about bad faith applies here. Bad faith is when you lie to yourself, when you collapse into the role others expect or rehearse an identity because it feels safer than freedom. Sartre's example was the waiter who plays at being nothing but a waiter, the spouse who hides behind duty, or the leader who exerts authority rather than inhabiting responsibility.[102]

In bad faith, you outsource your integrity to the audience, letting their applause stand in for your own coherence. But integrity doesn't live in performance. It lives in the unseen wrestling with conscience and the quiet moment when no one is looking and no one is clapping.

Each time you return to alignment and obscurity, you refuse bad faith. You reject the temptation to be defined by others and instead author yourself through fidelity between word and deed. That's why integrity loops are not grand. They're grounded. They don't protect you from anxiety or ambiguity. They honor them. They keep you from drifting into performance by demanding that your yes and no remain a matter of conscience, not convenience.

Integrity loops free you from the exhausting cycle of performance. They release you from the need to dramatize your cuts. Each loop closes the gap between who you say you are and how you actually live. Each loop makes it harder for the ghost of old identities to reclaim you. Integrity is not perfection; it's practice. It's the wrestle of conscience lived again and again until your yes and your no form a rhythm that belongs to you.

BECOME SOMEONE WORTH RETURNING TO

Each time you practice that fidelity in the present, you are also practicing fidelity to your future self. Every act of integrity is a down payment on the person you are becoming. Every yes or no made as a matter of conscience strengthens the ground your future self will stand on. When you align word and deed today, you give the gift of coherence to the one you will be tomorrow. Integrity, then, is not only loyalty to who you are now; it is loyalty to who you are becoming.

CRAFT YOUR PERSONAL RETURN CUE

As we've seen, becoming isn't grand. It's grounded, and grounded becoming requires rhythm. But rhythm is fragile. Drift is relentless. Comfort whispers daily. Ghosts tug constantly. Without an anchor, you will forget. That's why you need a return cue. A cue is not a performance. It's not a motivational mantra you post on your wall.

A true cue is personal, embodied, and repeatable. It's a practice that reminds you of who you are becoming in the moments when you're most likely to forget. That is where the Conscious Cut filters matter most. They keep your cue from collapsing into performance. A real cue brings you back to coherence, not convenience. It brings you back to fidelity, not applause.

Meaning is lived through the body, through presence, and through the way the world discloses itself to us in real time. A return cue must therefore be the following:

- **EMBODIED:** Something to do with your body, not just think with your mind

- **SITUATED:** Something that shows up in the everyday, not just in special settings

THE RECURRENCE EFFECT

- **RELATIONAL:** Something that orients you toward coherence with others, not just in solitude
- **REPEATABLE:** Not a one-time event but a rhythm you can lean on again and again

Here are some examples of cues to consider as you craft your own return cue, each grounded, embodied, and filtered for coherence.

- **BREATH CUE:** Each time you feel the pull of an old role, pause for one conscious breath and feel your feet on the floor and your expanded chest. The breath becomes a cut through comfort, returning you to clarity.
- **GESTURE CUE:** Create a small physical gesture—touching your wrist, pressing thumb and forefinger together, putting your hand over your heart. That should be a cue you can repeat daily with integrity—not performance, not applause, just fidelity.
- **PHRASE CUE:** Choose a sentence you whisper when drift shows up—"I return to what matters—fidelity not performance" or "This choice belongs to my becoming." The test is whether you'll still say it if no one hears it.
- **PLACE CUE:** Anchor yourself to a physical space—a chair, a bench, or a quiet room. Each time you step there, let it call you back. The question isn't "Am I being productive here?" but "Am I aligned here?"
- **RELATIONAL CUE:** Have a trusted witness check in with one question: "Where did you return this week?" Their presence cues your fidelity, not to what you achieve but to who you're becoming.

The key is not which cue you choose but whether it brings you back to coherence. Your return cue is how you stay faithful—not to performance, not to appearances, but to the self. You're authoring in rhythm because coherence is not proven once. It's practiced daily, and every time you activate your cue, you're not just returning to yourself *now*. You're practicing fidelity to your future self.

RETURN FROM THE DRIFT

Your return cue is not small. It is fidelity embodied. It is the reminder that becoming doesn't require reinvention but rhythm—that you don't need to be spectacular; you just need to be steady.

👁 AWAKEN

- Where are you still confusing repetition with return?
- What ordinary act of fidelity have you been underestimating?

📍 REMEMBER

- Becoming worth returning is not about arrival; it's about rhythm.
- Your smallest acts of coherence carry the greatest consequence.

THE RECURRENCE EFFECT

← RETURN

- What cue will you create to call yourself back when drift pulls you away?
- How will you practice fidelity to your future self in one act today?

The return isn't the end. It's the rhythm. You've cut. You've chosen. You've let go. You've walked through the fire, and you've learned that every cut has a cost, that clarity burns, that coherence requires grief, and that ashes are not an ending but a beginning.

Editing was never about perfection. It was never about arriving at some polished final version of yourself. It has always been about coherence—living in fidelity to what you see, even when it costs you comfort, applause, and old versions of yourself. But coherence isn't won once; it is sustained through return.

Nietzsche was right when he said, "You must be ready to burn yourself in your own flame. How could you rise anew if you have not first become ashes?"[103] The rise is not a single event; it's a rhythm. Each return is another rising. Each act of fidelity to your future self is another step out of the fire.

That is why the Conscious Cut filters matter to keep you honest. They're the guardrails against drift—the thresholds that prove whether you're returning to coherence or just rehearsing performance.

- **CLARITY > COMFORT:** Return to what is true, not what is easy.
- **COST > CONVENIENCE:** Return to what asks something of you. If it doesn't cost you, it won't change you.

BECOME SOMEONE WORTH RETURNING TO

- **WORTH RETURNING TO:** Return to rhythms you'd be proud to repeat, not impulses you'll regret.

- **AGENCY > APPROVAL:** Return to authorship, not performance for the crowd.

- **ALIGNMENT > ACHIEVEMENT:** Return to coherence with your becoming, not hollow success.

These filters cut through illusion. They remind you that every yes and no is a matter of conscience. They test whether your cuts are performance or liberation and whether you're drifting back into the familiar or authoring something coherent.

Life is lived in the everyday—in embodied gestures, small acts, and unseen choices. Integrity isn't built in declarations but in the quiet fidelity of return. Each loop between word and deed deepens coherence until it becomes a rhythm you can inhabit without apology.

This is the work ahead—not chasing novelty, not dramatizing reinvention, and not clinging to ghosts. The work is rhythm. The work is return because what you return to, you become. This is not the end of Editing. It is the beginning of fidelity.

I'll leave you with this. Will you live your return—guided by clarity, paid for with cost, aligned with coherence, faithful to your future self—even when no one's watching?

That's what it means to become someone worth returning to.

AFTERWORD
LONGING, DISCOVERY, AND RECKONING

If you want to build a ship, don't drum up the men to gather wood, divide the work, and give orders. Instead, teach them to yearn for the vast and endless sea.

ANTOINE DE SAINT-EXUPÉRY

This book was never meant to hand you lumber and blueprints. It is not a manual for better woodpiles. The world already has enough of those. What you need is not a formula but a hunger—not tasks but longing.

Without longing, drift wins. Drift whispers comfort, offers applause, and promises safety. Drift lets you keep stacking wood—busy and important but never awake. Longing is the ache that calls you beyond drift—beyond safety—into immensity.

Here is the turn most miss: Longing is not about goals. Goals are terminal states. You achieve them or you don't, and either way, you're left hollow. Achieve them, and the satisfaction evaporates quickly—just another summit with nothing but another peak waiting behind it. Miss them, and you collapse into shame, convinced that you've failed. This is the emotional roller-coaster of achievement: brief highs, punishing lows, endless chasing.

THE RECURRENCE EFFECT

Longing is different. Longing is perspective. Longing is intention. It isn't about a finish line but about what you orient toward, again and again. It doesn't collapse when a goal is reached because it was never about arriving. It sustains because it's about returning.

Antoine de Saint-Exupéry understood this.[104] Building ships isn't about the lumber. It's about the perspective that sees beyond the harbor, the intention to move toward immensity. Once you long for the sea, the daily choice—the small returns—align themselves with that horizon.

Albert Camus sharpens this truth with his image of Sisyphus. Condemned to roll the rock forever, Sisyphus is the anti-goal "hero." There is no terminal state, no final summit, and no achievement to check off. By every conventional measure, his task is futile, and yet Camus insists, "The struggle itself is enough to fill a man's heart. One must imagine Sisyphus happy."[105]

Why happy? It's because meaning does not live at the finish line. It lives in the return. Each push is a choice—not a choice Sisyphus asked for but one he makes his own. His burden is not done *to* him. It is done *for* him—the context in which his freedom emerges.

This is the reframe: You don't get to choose every rock you push. Illness, betrayal, loss, uncertainty—you didn't ask for them. But you do choose how to carry them. You choose whether to push asleep or awake. You choose whether to treat life as happening *to you* or *for you*.

That choice is the difference between drift and return. Drift says, *This isn't fair. This isn't what I wanted.* Return says, *It may not be the choice I wanted, but it is the choice I have. And I will meet it awake.*

Longing is what makes this possible. Longing reframes the struggle, not as punishment but as possibility—not as futility but as freedom. It is longing that transforms Sisyphus from a figure of despair into one of defiance, even joy.

LONGING, DISCOVERY, AND RECKONING

So yes, life is heavy. But if Sisyphus can be imagined as happy, so can you—not happy because the rock is easy, not happy because the hill is fair, but happy because the struggle is yours, because you are free to choose how you push.

That is the heart of longing—to desire a life lived awake, even when the rock rolls back again tomorrow.

The question is not whether you will struggle. You will. The question is this: *Will you see it as punishment or as a possibility? Will you drift through it asleep or return to it awake?*

DISCOVERY

I do not accept any absolute formulas for living. No preconceived code can see ahead to everything that can happen in a man's life. As we live, we grow and our beliefs change. They must change. So I think we should live with this constant discovery. We should be open to this adventure in heightened awareness of living. We should stake our whole existence on our willingness to explore and experience.

MARTIN BUBER

Longing points us beyond woodpiles and finish lines, but longing alone is not enough. Left untested, longing becomes fantasy. Buber reminds us that life is not about clinging to formulas.[106] It is about risking yourself in the adventure of discovery—an adventure that never ends.

That is why the rhythm of return matters. E4—Explore, Experiment, Evaluate, Edit—is not a checklist. It is not a closed system. It is a rhythm that invites discovery—a rhythm that insists you remain awake.

- **EXPLORE** forces you to see what drift has hidden. It is the discipline of awareness, the mirror that shows you what you'd rather avoid.

- **EXPERIMENT** demands courage. It's not theorizing about what might work. It's acting without a net, embracing the valley of despair as part of the process.

- **EVALUATE** asks you to resist your craving for immediate clarity. It requires patience to sit with dissonance, to let meaning emerge in its own time.

- **EDIT** is the courage to cut, to relinquish what no longer fits, even when it costs you comfort, belonging, or approval.

And then you do it again—not once, not twice, but as a rhythm—as long as you are alive.

Buber is right: There can be no absolute formula because life will always throw you into new terrain. Drift takes new forms. Challenges mutate. Losses arrive unannounced. If you cling to fixed codes, you will shatter when life refuses to conform.

But if you live as an explorer, discovery becomes the constant. You stop demanding that life be predictable. You stop chasing formulas to guarantee outcomes. Instead, you place your existence on willingness itself—to Explore, to Experiment, to Evaluate, to Edit, and to return.

Discovery is not a group project. Others can witness you, accompany you, and mirror you, but they cannot walk your path. As Nietzsche wrote, "No one can build you the bridge on which you, and only you, must cross the river of life. . . . There is one path in the world that none can walk but you. Where does it lead? Don't ask, walk!"[107]

LONGING, DISCOVERY, AND RECKONING

There is a river only you can cross, a bridge only you can step onto. To wait for certainty before moving is to never move at all. Where does it lead? Don't ask. Walk.

This is the scandal and the gift of recurrence. No one can return for you. No one can cut away for you. No one can step into your drift on your behalf. You must do it yourself, again and again.

Buber gives us openness. Nietzsche gives us authorship. Together they reveal the paradox: You are not given a map, but you are given freedom—no formulas and no guarantees but only a rhythm, a willingness, and your one path across the river.

Stake your existence on that willingness. Walk. Return. Become.

RECKONING

Tell me, what else should I have done? Doesn't everything die at last, and too soon? Tell me, what is it you plan to do with your one wild and precious life?

MARY OLIVER

Everything ends. That is the condition we live under but rarely face. Time is not generous. Every life, no matter how full, arrives at its end "too soon." You don't get to rehearse. You don't get to pause. Oliver's questions are not gentle. They are not an invitation to daydream. They are a call to awaken and begin taking authorship of your life.[108]

"What is it you plan to do with your one wild and precious life?"

The temptation is to postpone the answer—to tell yourself you'll live differently when things calm down, when the timing is

THE RECURRENCE EFFECT

right, and when you feel ready. But you already know that day never comes. Drift thrives on delay, and delay is itself a choice—the choice to bury what matters under busyness, woodpiles, and applause.

Seneca exposes this lie of delay: "It is not that we have a short time to live, but that we waste a lot of it. . . . Life is long if you know how to use it."[109]

We tell ourselves the tragedy is scarcity: *There isn't enough time.* But the tragedy is not that life is short. The tragedy is that we squander what we have. We live distracted. We scatter ourselves in trivial pursuits. We call busyness productivity. We call drift responsibility. Only when death confronts us do we realize we have been absent from our own lives. Death serves as the greatest clarifier, but even when it happens around us, we allow the world to draw us back into the busyness that numbs us.

Seneca's warning dismantles our excuses. The problem is not supply but stewardship. We are not powerless. We are wasteful, and waste is a choice.

Mary Oliver shows us the fragility of life. Seneca shows us our waste of it. Together, they leave us cornered—no appeals left, no escape hatch, no second life.

Nietzsche presses the blade deeper with his thought experiment of eternal recurrence: Imagine your life exactly as you are living it now, repeated forever. Would that be a blessing or a curse? Would you shudder in regret, or would you embrace the recurrence as a rhythm worth repeating?[110]

This is the core of the reckoning: What you are doing right now, you are becoming. If your days are full of drift, you will be adrift. If your days are anchored in return, your life will be coherent.

Camus insisted that we must imagine Sisyphus happy—not because the rock vanished but because he chose to see the struggle as his own. Oliver and Seneca insist that we must imagine ourselves awake—not because life is long or fair but because every moment wasted is one we will never return to.

Ask yourself these questions:

- What is worth returning to when everything else fades?
- What bridges will you regret not crossing when time finally runs out?
- If your life were to recur endlessly, would you want to live this version again?

Mortality is not here to terrify you. It is here to sober you—to remind you that your life is not measured in years but in returns. Death is what gives life meaning.

Oliver's question is the last mirror. Seneca's warning is the last push. Nietzsche and Camus close the circle: There is no avoiding struggle, no avoiding death, no avoiding choice.

Here is your choice:

- Bury it and suffer the dull ache of drift—a pain that numbs while it erodes.
- Carry it and suffer the sharp weight of awareness—a pain that unsettles but shapes.

Carrying does not guarantee ease. It guarantees struggle. But it also guarantees authorship. Burying may shield you from the sight of the rock, but it doesn't stop it from grinding you down in silence. Carrying means pushing awake, choosing your return, and living a life you would be willing to repeat.

One leads to drift, regret, and the slow erosion of your existence. The other leads to coherence, freedom, and a life that, while not easy, is worth returning to.

THE RECURRENCE EFFECT

So yes—carry it or bury it. But do not lie to yourself about where each road leads.

What you long for you return to, and what you return to you become. If this life were yours to live again and again, exactly as it is—would you be willing to carry it?

Tell me—and more importantly, tell yourself—what will you do with your one wild and precious life?

EPILOGUE
THE END OF THE BEGINNING

This is not the end. It is not even the beginning of the end. But it is perhaps the end of the beginning.

WINSTON CHURCHILL

N ow you stand here at the threshold—not finished, not even close. You've stood in the mirror. You've seen the choice. There is nothing left to explain. There is only this: The step you take next will echo.

There are no safe paths, only honest ones. There are no formulas, only returns. There is no way to escape the cost, only the decision of whether you will pay it awake or asleep.

To bury it is to suffer the slow rot of drift. To carry it is to suffer the sharp weight of return.

Either way, there will be pain. That much is unavoidable. The only choice you have is which pain will be yours.

If you need to be reminded of the cost, hear American writer and civil rights activist James Baldwin: "I do not mean to be sentimental about suffering . . . but people who cannot suffer can never grow up, can never discover who they are."[111]

THE RECURRENCE EFFECT

If you need to be reminded of the freedom, hear American existential-humanist therapist James F. T. Bugental: "Our true identity is a process, not a substantive thing. Thus we are continually changing. The effort to remain unchanging is crippling and results in a smaller life."[112]

One voice tells you the road will hurt. The other tells you the road will change you.

Both are true.

Regardless of which mirror you choose to carry, remember this: It is not about being the strongest. It is about choosing to move forward no matter how small the step. You are never finished—not until your last breath. That means that today, tomorrow, and every day until the end, you can choose again.

So step. Return. Become.

Always remember what Camus told us, "The struggle itself towards the heights is enough to fill a man's heart. One must imagine Sisyphus happy."[113]

NOTES

1. Alicia Nortje, "What Is Cognitive Bias? 7 Examples & Resources (Incl. Codex)," *PositivePsychology*, August 5, 2020, https://positivepsychology.com/cognitive-biases.

2. Jason N. Linder, "The Overlooked and Misunderstood Arrival Fallacy," *Psychology Today*, March 28, 2025, https://www.psychologytoday.com/us/blog/mindfulness-insights/202503/the-overlooked-and-misunderstood-arrival-fallacy.

3. Herbert Spiegelberg and Walter Biemel, "Phenomenology," *Britannica Online*, s.v., accessed June 11, 2025, https://www.britannica.com/topic/phenomenology.

4. American Psychological Association, "Existential Phenomenology," *APA Dictionary of Psychology*, s.v., accessed June 11, 2025, https://dictionary.apa.org/existential-phenomenology.

5. Friedrich Nietzsche, "Schopenhauer as Educator," in *Nietzsche: Untimely Meditations*, ed. Daniel Breazeale, trans. R. J. Hollingdale (Cambridge: Cambridge University Press, 1997), 125–94.

6. Saul McLeod, "Maslow's Hierarchy of Needs," *Simply Psychology*, March 14, 2025, https://www.simplypsychology.org/maslow.html.

7. Martin Heidegger, *Being and Time* (Albany: State University of New York Press, 1996), 120.

8. Søren Kierkegaard, *The Sickness unto Death,* trans. Edna Hatlestad Hong and Howard Vincent Hong (Princeton: Princeton University Press, 1980), 32–33.

9. Evan M. Gordon, Roselyne J. Chauvin, Andrew N. Van, et al., "A Somato-Cognitive Action Network Alternates with Effector Regions in Motor Cortex," *Nature* 617 (2023), 351–359, https://doi.org/10.1038/s41586-023-05964-2.

10. Maurice Merleau-Ponty, *Phenomenology of Perception*, trans. Colin Smith (London: Routledge & Kegan Paul, 1962), xvi–xvii.

NOTES

11 Molly McDonough, "Making Sense of Interoception," *Harvard Medicine*, Spring 2024, https://magazine.hms.harvard.edu/articles/making-sense-interoception.

12 Rainer Maria Rilke, *Letters to a Young Poet*, trans. Stephen Mitchell (New York: Random House, 1984), 34.

13 Anaïs Nin, *The Diary of Anaïs Nin*, Vol. 1: 1931–1934 (New York: Houghton Mifflin Harcourt Publishing Company, 1966), 126.

14 Paul B. Armstrong, *Stories and the Brain: The Neuroscience of Narrative* (Baltimore: Johns Hopkins University Press, 2020).

15 Friedrich Nietzsche, *On the Genealogy of Morals: A Polemic*, trans. Michael A Scarpitti (London: Penguin Classics, 2013), 1.

16 Rhoshel K. Lenroot and Jay N. Giedd, "Sex Differences in the Adolescent Brain," *Brain and Cognition* 72, no. 1 (2010): 46–55, doi:10.1016/j.bandc.2009.10.008.

17 Jean-Paul Sartre, *Existentialism and Human Emotions* (New York: Citadel Press, 1957), 15.

18 Rollo May, *Man's Search for Himself* (New York: W.W. Norton & Company, Inc., 1953), 169.

19 Rainer Maria Rilke, *Letters to a Young Poet*, trans. Stephen Mitchell (New York: Random House, 1984), 34.

20 Hector Garcia and Francesc Miralles, *The Book of Ichigo Ichie: The Art of Making the Most of Every Moment, the Japanese Way*, trans. Charlotte Whittle (New York: Penguin Books, 2019), 3.

21 Martin Heidegger, *Being and Time* (Albany: State University of New York Press, 1996).

22 Simone Weil, "April 13, 1942 Letter to Friend and Poet Joë Bousquet," in *Correspondance* (Lausanne: Editions l'Age d'Homme, 1982), 18.

23 *The Secret Life of Walter Mitty*, directed by Ben Stiller (2013, Los Angeles: Twentieth Century Fox).

24 Søren Kierkegaard, *Either/Or: A Fragment of Life*, trans. Alastair Hannay (London: Penguin Books, 1992), 214.

25 Maurice Merleau-Ponty, *Phenomenology of Perception*, trans. Colin Smith (London: Routledge & Kegan Paul, 1962), 203.

26 Irvin D. Yalom, *Existential Psychotherapy* (New York: Basic Books, 1980), 40.

27 Thich Nhat Hanh, *Peace Is Every Step: The Path of Mindfulness in Everyday Life* (New York: Bantam Books, 1990), 21.

28 José Ortega y Gasset, *Mission of the University*, trans. Howard Lee Nostrand (New Brunswick: Transaction Publishers, 2009), 63.

29 Teal Burrell, "Why Dopamine Drives You to Do Hard Things—Even Without a Reward," *National Geographic*, May 15, 2024, https://www.nationalgeographic.com/science/article/dopamine-motivation-reward-system.

30 Maurice Merleau-Ponty, *Phenomenology of Perception*, trans. Colin Smith (London: Routledge & Kegan Paul, 1962), 129.

31 Søren Kierkegaard, *The Concept of Anxiety: A Simple Psychologically Orienting Deliberation on the Dogmatic Issue of Hereditary Sin*, trans. Reidar Thomte (Princeton: Princeton University Press, 1980), 61.

32 Jean-Paul Sartre, *La Nausée* (Paris: Éditions Gallimard, 1938).

33 Simone de Beauvoir, *The Ethics of Ambiguity*, trans. Bernard Frechtman (New York: Open Road Integrated Media, 2018), 24.

34 Friedrich Nietzsche, *The Portable Nietzsche*, trans. Walter Kaufmann (New York: Viking Penguin Inc., 1954), 468.

35 *The Office*, Season 4, Episode 4, directed by Paul Lieberstein (October 18, 2007; New York: Peacock).

36 Neel Burton, "Jean-Paul Sartre's Bad Faith: The Danger of Denying Freedom," *Psychology Today*, October 17, 2023, https://www.psychologytoday.com/us/blog/hide-and-seek/202310/jean-paul-sartres-bad-faith-the-danger-of-denying-freedom.

NOTES

37 Albert Camus, *The Rebel: An Essay on Man in Revolt*, trans. Anthony Bower (New York: Vintage International, 1991), 304.

38 Eleanor Roosevelt, *You Learn by Living: Eleven Keys for a More Fulfilling Life* (New York: Harper, 1960), 30.

39 *The Matrix*, directed by Lana Wachowski and Lilly Wachowski (1999, Burbank, CA: Warner Bros.).

40 Martin Buber, *I and Thou*, trans. Ronald Gregor Smith (New York: Charles Scribner's Sons, 1958), 25.

41 Maurice Merleau-Ponty, *Phenomenology of Perception*, trans. Colin Smith (London: Routledge & Kegan Paul, 1962), lxxxii.

42 *The Matrix*, directed by Lana Wachowski and Lilly Wachowski (1999, Burbank, CA: Warner Bros.).

43 Martin Heidegger, *Being and Time* (Albany: State University of New York Press, 1996), 120.

44 Simone de Beauvoir, *The Second Sex*, trans. Constance Borde and Sheila Malovany-Chevallair (New York: Penguin Random House, 2009), 283.

45 W. E. B. Du Bois, *Dusk of Dawn* (Chicago: Harcourt, Brace & World, Inc, 1940), 63.

46 Maurice Merleau-Ponty, *Phenomenology of Perception,* trans. Colin Smith (London: Routledge & Kegan Paul, 1962), 396.

47 Maurice Merleau-Ponty, *Phenomenology of Perception*, trans. Colin Smith (London: Routledge & Kegan Paul, 1962), 456.

48 Simone de Beauvoir, *All Said and Done*, trans. Patrick O'Brian (New York: Putnam, 1974), 16.

49 Gabriel García Márquez, *Love in the Time of Cholera*, trans. Edith Grossman (New York: Alfred A. Knopf, 1997), 199.

50 A. W. Kruglanski and D. M. Webster, "Motivated Closing of the Mind: 'Seizing' and 'Freezing,'" *Psychological Review* 103, no. 2 (1992): 263–83, https://doi.org/10.1037/0033-295X.103.2.263.

51 Paul Tillich, *The Courage to Be* (New Haven: Yale University Press, 1952), 164.

52 José Ortega y Gasset, *The Revolt of the Masses*, authorized translation (New York: W.W. Norton & Company, Inc., 1932), 12.

53 Rollo May, *Freedom and Destiny* (New York: Dell Publishing Co., Inc., 1981), 5.

54 Karl Jaspers, *Tragedy Is Not Enough*, trans. Harald Reiche, Harry Moore, and Karl Deutsch (Boston: The Beacon Press, 1952), 104.

55 Alfred Korzybski, *Science and Sanity. An Introduction to Non-Aristotelian Systems and General Semantics* (New York: Institute of General Semantics, 1933), 747–61.

56 Fyodor Dostoevsky, *The Brothers Karamazov*, trans. Constance Garnet (New York: The Macmillan Company, 1922), 40.

57 Anne-Laure Le Cunff, "Your Brain on Uncertainty," *Ness Labs*, accessed August 28, 2025, https://nesslabs.com/your-brain-on-uncertainty-neuroscience.

58 Jean-Paul Sartre, *Essays in Existentialism* (New York: Citadel Press, 1965), 54.

59 *Etymonline*, s.v. "courage," accessed August 28, 2025, https://www.etymonline.com/word/courage.

60 Dan W. Grupe and Jack B. Nitschke, "Uncertainty and Anticipation in Anxiety: An Integrated Neurobiological and Psychological Perspective," *Nature Reviews*, Neuroscience 14, no. 7 (2013): 488–501, doi:10.1038/nrn3524.

61 Kendra Cherry, "How Neuroplasticity Works," *Very Well Mind*, May 17, 2024, https://www.verywellmind.com/what-is-brain-plasticity-2794886.

62 Henry David Thoreau, *Journal XII*, April 23, 1859, https://www.walden.org/work/journal-xii-march-2-1859-november-30-1859/.

63 Irvin D. Yalom, *When Nietzsche Wept* (New York: HarperCollins Publishers, 1992), 179.

NOTES

64 G. W. F. Hegel, *The Phenomenology of Mind*, trans. J.B. Baillie (New York: Macmillan Company, 1931), 16.

65 Albert Camus, "October 1952," in *Notebooks* 1951–1951, trans. Ryan Bloom (Chicago: Ivan R. Dee, 2008).

66 Carl Rogers, *On Becoming a Person: A Therapist's View of Psychotherapy* (Boston: Houghton Mifflin, 1961), 122.

67 Benjamin Hardy, *Personality Isn't Permanent* (New York: Portfolio, 2020).

68 Ellen Langer, *The Power of Mindful Learning* (Boston: Merloyd Lawrence, 2016), 126.

69 Benjamin Hardy, *Personality Isn't Permanent* (New York: Portfolio, 2020), 101.

70 Carl Rogers, *On Becoming a Person* (New York: Mariner Books, 2012).

71 Jennifer Kretchmar, "Social Learning Theory," *EBSCO*, accessed September 3, 2025, https://www.ebsco.com/research-starters/education/social-learning-theory.

72 Benjamin Hardy, *Willpower Doesn't Work: Discover the Hidden Keys to Success* (New York: Hachette Books, 2018).

73 Carl Rogers, *On Becoming a Person* (New York: Mariner Books, 2012), 283.

74 Marcia B. Baxter Magolda, "Self-Authorship," *New Directions for Higher Education* 2014, no. 166 (2014): 25–33, https://doi.org/10.1002/he.20092.

75 Edmund Husserl, *The Basic Problems of Phenomenology*, trans. Ingo Farin and James Hart (Dordrecht: Springer, 2006), 107.

76 Cecilia Lucero, "Provocative Moments in Advising: Guiding Students Toward Self-Authorship," *NACADA*, February 26, 2018, https://nacada.ksu.edu/Resources/Academic-Advising-Today/View-Articles/Provocative-Moments-in-Advising-Guiding-Students-Toward-Self-Authorship.aspx.

THE RECURRENCE EFFECT

77 Daniel Kahneman, *Thinking Fast and Slow* (New York: Farrar, Straus and Giroux, 2011), 62.

78 Maurice Merleau-Ponty, *Phenomenology of Perception*, trans. Colin Smith (London: Routledge & Kegan Paul, 1962), xxii.

79 Carl Jung, *The Wisdom of Carl Jung*, ed. Edward Hoffman (New York: Citadel Press Books, 2003), 109.

80 Mihaly Csikszentmihalyi, *Flow: The Psychology of Optimal Experience* (New York: Springer, 2014), 257.

81 David Gal and Derek D. Rucker, "The Loss of Loss Aversion: Will It Loom Larger Than Its Gain?" *Journal of Consumer Psychology* 28, no. 3 (2018): 497–516.

82 Søren Kierkegaard, *The Concept of Anxiety*, trans. Reidar Thomte (Princeton: Princeton University Press, 1980), 61.

83 Kirk J. Schneider, *The Paradoxical Self: Toward an Understanding of Our Contradictory Nature* (London: Bloomsbury Academic, 1999), 7.

84 Michelle Sibol, "When Life Changes, We Grieve: Holding Ourselves Gently Through Transition," *Integrated Care Clinic*, May 20, 2025, https://integratedcareclinic.com/blog/when-life-changes-we-grieve-holding-ourselves-gently-through-transition/.

85 John Sweller, "Cognitive Load Theory and Individual Differences," *Learning and Individual Differences* 110, February 2024, https://doi.org/10.1016/j.lindif.2024.102423.

86 Hanneke E. M. den Ouden, Peter Kok, and Floris P. de Lange, "How Prediction Errors Shape Perception, Attention, and Motivation," *Frontiers in Psychology* 3, December 10, 2012, https://doi.org/10.3389/fpsyg.2012.00548.

87 Faith Jeremiah, Russell Butson, and Adekunle Oke, "New Perspectives on Repetitive Behaviour," *Psychological Research* 89, no. 261 (March 6, 2025), doi:10.1007/s00426-025-02092-6.

88 Simone de Beauvoir, *All Said and Done* (New York: Marlowe, 1994), 16.

NOTES

89 Dan Pilat and Sekoul Krastev, "Hebbian Learning," *The Decision Lab*, accessed September 22, 2025, https://thedecisionlab.com/reference-guide/neuroscience/hebbian-learning.

90 Blair Paley and Nastassia J. Hajal, "Conceptualizing Emotion Regulation and Coregulation as Family-Level Phenomena," *Clinical Child and Family Psychology Review* 25, no. 1 (2022): 19–43, doi:10.1007/s10567-022-00378-4.

91 "Understanding the Stress Response," *Harvard Health Publishing*, April 3, 2024, https://www.health.harvard.edu/staying-healthy/understanding-the-stress-response.

92 Charles Bukowski, *What Matters Most Is How Well You Walk Through the Fire* (New York: Ecco, 2002).

93 Sharon Vaisvaser, "The Embodied-Enactive-Interactive Brain: Bridging Neuroscience and Creative Arts Therapies," *Frontiers in Psychology* 12 (April 28, 2021), https://doi.org/10.3389/fpsyg.2021.634079.

94 Friedrich Nietzsche, *Thus Spoke Zarathustra*, trans. Walter Kaufmann (New York: Penguin Books, 1978), 64.

95 Dermot Moran, "Being-with (Mitsein)," in *The Cambridge Heidegger Lexicon*, ed. Mark A. Wrathall (Cambridge: Cambridge University Press, 2021), 111–5, https://doi.org/10.1017/9780511843778.025.

96 Maurice Merleau-Ponty, *Phenomenology of Perception*, trans. Colin Smith (London: Routledge & Kegan Paul, 1962), 129.

97 Maurice Merleau-Ponty, *Phenomenology of Perception*, trans. Colin Smith (London: Routledge & Kegan Paul, 1962), 203.

98 Martin Heidegger, "Building Dwelling Thinking," in *Poetry, Language, Thought* (New York: Harper & Row, 1971), 143–61.

99 Søren Kierkegaard, *The Present Age*, trans. Alexander Dru (New York: Harper Perennial, 1962).

THE RECURRENCE EFFECT

100 Nick Cave, "I Love the Song Night Raid," *The Red Hand Files*, December 2022, https://www.theredhandfiles.com/i-love-the-song-night-raid/.

101 Friedrich Nietzsche, *The Portable Nietzsche*, trans. Walter Kaufmann, (New York: Viking Press, 1954), 632.

102 Jean-Paul Sartre, *Essays in Existentialism* (New York: Citadel Press, 1965), 54.

103 Friedrich Nietzsche, *Thus Spoke Zarathustra*, trans. Walter Kaufmann (New York: Penguin Books, 1978), 64.

104 Antoine de Saint-Exupéry, "Citadelle," in *Oeuvres* (Paris: Gallimard, 1959), 687.

105 Albert Camus, *The Myth of Sisyphus*, trans. Justin O'Brien (New York: Vintage International, 1955), 123.

106 Aubrey Hodes, Martin Buber: *An Intimate Portrait* (New York: Viking Press, 1971), 56.

107 Friedrich Nietzsche, "Schopenhauer as Educator," in *Nietzsche: Untimely Meditations*, ed. Daniel Breazeale, trans. R. J. Hollingdale (Cambridge: Cambridge University Press, 1997), 125–94.

108 Mary Oliver, "Poem 133: The Summer Day," in *New and Selected Poems* (Boston: Beacon Press, 1992).

109 Seneca, *On the Shortness of Life*, trans. C. D. N. Costa (New York Penguin Books, 2005), 1–2.

110 Friedrich Nietzsche, *The Gay Science*, trans. Thomas Common (New York: Dover Publications, Inc. 2006).

111 James Baldwin, *The Fire Next Time* (New York: Vintage International, 1993), 98.

112 James F. T. Bugental, *Intimate Journeys* (San Francisco: Jossey-Bass, 1990), 326.

113 Albert Camus, *The Myth of Sisyphus*, trans. Justin O'Brien (New York: Vintage International, 1955), 123.

www.ingramcontent.com/pod-product-compliance
Lightning Source LLC
LaVergne TN
LVHW020431070526
838199LV00025B/597/J